The Diary of Princess Pushy's Sister

A MEMOIR (PART 1)

Samantha Markle

CENTRAL PARK SOUTH PUBLISHING

Publisher: Central Park South Publishing

Website: www.centralparksouthpublishing.com

Publisher's Note - This is a work of non-fiction.

Book Layout and Cover Design – Mark Mázers/alienartifacts

The Diary of Princess Pushy's Sister by **Samantha Markle © 2021**. -- 1st ed.

ISBN 978-1-7363134-1-1

Dedication

I dedicate this book in loving memory to grandmother, Doris Sanders Markle whose strength, self-sacrifice and optimism, made it possible for our family to grow and overcome whatever challenges life hands us. I also dedicate this to my father, Thomas W. Markle, whose love and dedication made it possible for me, Meg, and my brother Tom Jr., to have a very full and blessed life, always reminding us of our strengths, guiding us to discover new ones, and for helping me to find my wings when I couldn't walk.

To my dear friends Hyacinth and John, for their souls, wisdom, and eternal friendship. To Betty Gosling Wernom, for her love, and motherly advice over the years. I also want to thank people everyone who believed in me, when it was difficult to see through tabloid headlines.

This is my look back on my life since 1960s, growing up in a very extraordinary and normal family. It is a memoir of my personal experiences and observations, as a granddaughter, daughter, sister, mother, in a family that collided with history in an unexpected but relatable way.

Our lives have not always been easy, and no one is perfect. We have, laughed, agreed, disagreed, and forgiven each other, which is what makes families so special.

Contents

Markle Beginnings

My favorite grandmother, Doris Rita-May Sanders, (Grandma Markle), was born in Alton, New Hampshire in 1920 to Gertrude and Fred Sanders. Doris and her three brothers, Don, Carl, and Ralph went to church, enjoyed art, singing, and playing musical instruments. She was always very proud that her grandfather, George Merrill, was integral in the development of the New Hampshire rail road system. My grandmother noted in a memoir to me, that our family ascended from Captain John Smith of Ipswich England, who traveled during the Great Migration of 1632, from England to Nantasket, Massachusetts on the ship "Lyon," and King "Robert The Bruce" of Scotland, (13th generation, by direct lineage) and Benedict Arnold. Even at an early age, I knew that the family tree was scattered with brave and creative characters. My grandmother loved telling stories of our family tree, but in my heart, my family really began with my grandmother and my grandfather. Doris was jovial and very pretty, she was somewhat shy, and did not date until, she met Gordon A. Markle, on August 8th, 1941. He worked as a military policeman, and also as a parachute repair man. Gordon was first smitten by her sapphire blue eyes, timid but tempting smile, and pixie nose. Although she aspired to be an actress, Doris didn't have transportation to take acting classes that were far away, so she abandoned the idea, choosing instead, to have a family. Doris and Gordon were married on March,13, 1941.

The first home they purchased was a modest 3-bedroom home in Newport, Pennsylvania. There was plenty of room for the new family to grow there. Doris was maternal, and enjoyed spending every moment with Gordon that she could. She wanted a big family. Gordon was open to whatever she wanted.

Their new married family life was flowing smoothly, and they couldn't foresee anything interrupting their happy home, until the Japanese bombed Pearl Harbor on December 7th, of 1941. Gordon was called to duty at Hickam Field, Hawaii. Many men in town were called to duty, which required the women to take care of their families, with the help of other family members and friends. Doris knew that she could handle everything while he was gone, albeit with a bit of occasional help from friends, who were considered as welcomed to walk in at any time.

When Gordon returned from Hickam Field, he could finally settle into being a family man, and alleviate some of the routine monotony of running the household, which Doris had managed single-handedly in his absence. To make the house a home, they had three sons Michael, Frederick and Thomas who was born in July 1945. Doris had a feeling that he would bring something unique to the family tree someday.

Even as a baby, Thomas had a curiously expressive eyebrow that should have been trademarked, in his childhood, as a classic Markle trait, along with his slightly upturned nose. He was charming, and clean cut, with a twinkle in his eye, dimples in his cheeks, a slight gap in between his teeth, and an upturned nose.

The family tree was abundant with creative individuals, and since "apples don't fall far from the tree," as the old saying goes, it naturally followed that Thomas found his passion in the art of set and lighting design. By the time he was 18, he had become so good at his craft, that he set out for Chicago to get a job working in television. Luckily, he was hired to work at WTTW T.V., (a public broadcasting television station). Thomas was happy to be making enough money to support himself, as he worked his way up to being a lighting director. He kept in contact with his mother and father, to give them updates about his adventures in Chicago. Doris really wanted to be a grandmother, so although she was somewhat soft spoken, she had no problem firmly voicing her encouragement that her sons have children.

Although Thomas hadn't planned on settling down yet, a good

friend of his, whose sister he was fond of, suggested that he meet a female friend as a romantic possibility. Because he had his eye on his friend's sister, he declined the offer to meet the other woman.

Thomas' avoidance of the meeting was kiboshed by the arrangement of a "blind date" for him. He should have pretended that he had Dengue Fever, but instead he reluctantly agreed to the deal. Roslyn was 5 foot 9, had red hair, was not shy and was quite available. Although she was not his first preference, she would suffice for him, as he was a typical hormonally charged male.

Tom loved his work but also made time for Roslyn. They enjoyed each other's company, and he enjoyed the fact that she was promiscuous. In addition to being physically assertive, she was somewhat loud and boisterous. She was the complete opposite of his mother, who was generally soft spoken. Whatever it was about her that was so mesmerizing, he stopped seeing other women.

.

CHAPTER TWO

Ode to Little Surprises

1964 was a radically progressive year for the United States. President Lyndon Johnson signed the Civil Rights Act into law, at age 35, Martin Luther King Jr. received the Nobel Peace Prize for non-violent resistance to segregation in the United States, Muhammad Ali "floated like a butterfly, and stung like a bee," winning him the boxing world heavyweight championship, the price of a new house was only $13,000, a loaf of bread cost $.21, The Beatles refused to play for segregated audiences, and more of the United States was about to begin removing racial barriers.

As was the case for many men, it was also the year that Thomas received a notice in the mail, that he was being drafted into the Vietnam war. He was 6 feet tall, in moderately athletic shape, clean-shaven, and optimistic. He had an easy-going way, and like his mother, he seldom complained, even in uncomfortable situations, like standing in a long line of anxious, military draftees. As he looked around the room wondering what the lives of the other men might be like, he also worried about how military service might affect his own family life, and career plans. No matter what the case was, he was willing to serve his country, if he was called to do so.

He fumbled with his keys in his left pocket and held his draft application in the other hand. As he looked around at the other men in line, he took notice of a short, stocky young man with a nervous smile, who repeatedly stepped out of the line, and then stepped back into it. He looked at Thomas, and said, "I'm dying to go to Nam!" The word dying resonated through his body like a jackhammer. He felt his bravado waning, as his hands grew clammy, and his knees nearly gave out for a moment, but he masked it with a smile, and a stiff, compensating posture. The boxy little room was sweltering hot, which only intensified Thomas' uneasy feelings about war. Suddenly the front door of the building opened to allow for a rush of air to come through the door. Although the room cooled off a bit, it didn't make him feel any better. He looked back at the fellow and said, "Be careful what you wish for." The giddy young man winked and smiled, arrogantly. "Maybe you don't have the right stuff. I'm sure you can find a way out of it," he urged.

Thomas dismissed the conversation with a smirk, a furrowed brow, as he shuffled to the front of the line. Sitting at a long table, was a clean shaven, muscular man in his mid-forties, peering through a pair of heavy black rimmed glasses, as he read through a stack of papers. He looked up, raised his arm, and waved his hand, as he yelled "Next!" Nervously, Thomas stepped forward, and put his application on the table. "Thank you, son," the man mumbled. As he read over Thomas' application, he got out a handkerchief, and dabbed the perspiration off his forehead.

"What are you doing here?" he asked. "Well, Sir, I got a draft notice, and I'm here to serve my country," Thomas replied. The man shook his head a couple of times, and handed Thomas the application back. "Go home son. Kennedy doesn't want parents in the war. Your application here, says you have a baby on the way. Enjoy your family," the man said, as he pointed to the exit door. Thomas coughed to hide a gasp of relief. Just then, the young man behind him blurted out arrogantly, "I guess some people just have all the luck," as he hurried to the recruiter's desk. Thomas said, "You're right, I'm a father!" As if a ton of bricks had been lifted off of his shoulders, he walked hurriedly out the door, knowing that he would soon be a father. He was 19 years old, and he would be starting adult life with a jiffy pop family. Like a lot of families in the '60s, who came together quickly, either to avoid the draft, or because they were a family already in progress when the draft began, he knew he was taking on huge responsibilities. Little did he know that marriage and family life can be great, but it could also turn out to be as stressful as going to war. His life as a family man would take him in a direction personally, professionally, and historically, that he could not imagine. Tom and Roslyn didn't want to have a child out of wedlock, so they had a very simple marriage by the justice of the peace, and Thomas' mother couldn't be happier.

I was the blessed bun in the oven or the Golden Child who was causal in my father escaping the Vietnam war. If he went to war and made it back alive, he probably would not have not stayed with my mother, by his report, and would have met someone else. Most likely, he would have returned with a Vietnamese wife, like many soldiers did. Luckily for me, Thomas and Roslyn gave birth to me on November 24 of 1964.

I came into the world, like a speeding train with a megaphone attached to the front of it, and oblivious to the radical social change that was going on around me.

My brother was born 14 months after I was; in September of 1966. It was a good thing that our grandparents offered to help with anything they could, because my parents would definitely need the extra food and diaper money. Although my dad was doing well at his job, he didn't make a lot of money at first, so we took an apartment on the Southside of Chicago that was affordable.

Dad worked diligently, so that our little branch of the Markle family tree would grow into something hopefully discussion-worthy. He was sure that he could give my brother and I an abundant and colorful life.

I say, we took an apartment, but all my brother and I had to do, was make baby sounds, and drool. Dad was still working his way up at the studio, so he worked long hours, while my mother stayed home thinking he was having affairs.

That period went by quickly, and Dad progressed steadily up at his job, so within a couple of years, we moved to a great old brown stone building in North Chicago. Our apartment was on the bottom floor, and it appeared as though it had been perfectly cared for since it was built in the roaring '20s. It was divided up into two apartments because it was so large.

I remember the sprawling glazed wood floors, elaborate crown molding where the top of the wall meets the ceiling, and crystal door-knobs on every door, which were so characteristic of interior design in the 1920s. To give it even more flare, our very eccentric neighbors upstairs were Drag Queen nightclub performers, who made a regular practice of giving me all of their unwanted sequin and feather dresses. Needless to say, I was the most elegantly dressed first grader in the neighborhood, when it came time to play dress-up. I was only 6, but I had a wardrobe comparable to that of Liza Minnelli. The dresses made my home performances to albums such as Cabaret rather extravagant. I knew every song on the album and eventually choreographed my dance steps so well, that the dresses, feathers and sequins swayed to the beat of the music, as I sang and shimmied.

My social world gave me very early exposure to a wide variety of cultures and people. My early life lens was more like a kaleidoscope; colorful, in constant motion, and never the same, from one day to the next. Experiences like that gave me a very open approach to people and to life. After being a child in Chicago, I could never imagine a homogenous society. Because the TV station was a public broadcasting station, most of the programs I watched were educational and arts related. We watched television shows like *Soundstage, The Electric Company, The Masterpiece Theatre, Nova, Monty Python's Flying Circus*, and National Geographic shows.

My elementary school was composed of kids from every socioeconomic level, every skin color, and ethnicity. Because difference was the norm, nobody pointed out difference. The only differences we really paid attention to were what kids were wearing, and what was in our lunchboxes. I was one of those kids who associated memories around food. If we noticed any inequality, it was lunchbox inequality and most of us shared or traded for something we liked. It seemed as though there was always that one kid who had Twinkies, chips, fruit, and chocolate milk, instead of plain white milk and bologna sandwiches.

I never considered myself to be one of the popular kids, because, at that age, I was tall compared to most of the girls in my class, and I struggled with unmanageably wavy hair.

I had a snarky sense of humor, and had more fun clowning

around than I did worrying about what I looked like. I was generally happy go lucky. I was not judgmental of others, so I just assumed that others saw life through a similar lens. I generalized the eclectic world around me to be the entire world. That time in my life was carefree untainted by stereotypes, or biased attitudes.

CHAPTER THREE

When Grandma Said the "N" Word

There comes a time when the naïveté of childhood is challenged or adjusted by facts, social norms, and the opinions of others. My naïveté about social attitudes was first challenged by my mother's mother. My mother's mother, Grandma Loveless, did not live very far away from our apartment, so I walked to her house after school.

On the way to school one day, my friends and I passed a burned down apartment building. We stopped walking when we noticed a large tortoise that was struggling to crawl in the dirt near the side of the building.

It looked as though it had been burned. Aside from the fact it was burned, I was puzzled because I had never seen a turtle in Chicago, and we were nowhere near water. I was afraid to touch it, but my friend picked it up, and said, "Maybe we can save him." I thought that he was quite heroic, and I was impressed at what a big heart he had. A scruffy, grouchy old man, wearing a bathrobe, came over to us and yelled, "You kids put that down!" We didn't want to get in trouble, so my friend reluctantly put the turtle down, and we hurried to school. As I sat in class, I wondered throughout the day whether or not the turtle was still alive. After school, I hurried to my grandmother's house, and I couldn't wait to tell her about my day at school. It was often the best part of my day, because it involved a plate of my grandmother's homemade cookies.

I sat at the kitchen table anxiously dunking freshly baked, chewy, homemade chocolate chip cookies into a glass of milk, while my grandmother pasted S&H Green Stamps into the rows of perfectly linear spaces in the stamp book. It seemed as though everything in her kitchen was linear and purchased with the stamps, earned from items purchased that took part in the green stamp program. Routinely, she purchased participating products, accumulated more stamps, and then purchased more items.

Dorothy had a good job working as a secretary at the Federal Reserve Bank in Chicago, and she boasted regularly that she was quite a spendthrift. She "wasted not," and "wanted not." When I asked why she covered some of the furniture and collectible things in her house in plastic zip covers, she always said, "Well during the war, times were tough, food was being rationed, and we didn't know when we were going to get more, so we were frugal." I understood the concept of taking care of things, but I thought that preserving so many things in plastic covers or sheets, was a bit extreme. It didn't make sense to me, that she would spend good money on the furniture, only to cover it. I didn't ask what she did with her money, but she always bragged that she saved it. She often called herself Scotchy. When people asked what my ancestry was, I replied, "Scotchy, Irish, and English." Dorothy never traveled anywhere outside of the United States. Her idea of experiencing more of the world was watching National Geographic and Lawrence Welk on television. The TV show she was watching showed people sitting in gondolas going down some sort of tropical river. I asked her what she was doing for the day, and she sounded like she had just got back from vacation. She said, "Oh, I went to Brazil yesterday, and today I'm going to the Amazon." I thought she lived vicariously through television shows. She was not alone in her imaginary boat going down the Amazon river. Many of us lived vicariously through the television shows that took us around the world.

I think in many ways, she was able to revisit her youth through hearing about my adventures. She didn't interact with a lot of people socially, and I often wondered why. Oddly, she loved asking me what I did at school each day. I remember proudly telling her about my friend, whom I walked to school with one day, and that we found a giant turtle. I said, "Grandma, we found a turtle in that burned apartment building. My friend tried to save it." "What friend?" she asked. "My black friend," I boasted. Kids in our class normally described each other by basic physical traits. I was tall and had wavy hair. I had heard some describe me as that tall girl. None of the kids at school discriminated against each other based on physical characteristics, but we described each other that way. I didn't get to finish the sentence, before she raised her finger at me scoldingly, and said, "He will take you down an alley and rape you! Don't you talk to that boy!" She started mumbling under her breath and ended her rant with the "N-word." I didn't know what rape was, but by the tone of her voice, I thought it must be horrible. I had never heard the other word before either. I couldn't understand why she would say such a terrible thing about someone she didn't know, much less a little boy. "He's really nice Grandma, he's my friend, he wouldn't hurt anybody! He even tried to save a turtle," I uttered reluctantly. She looked at me without blinking her eyes, and said, "There will be no more talk about it." She shook her head, and continued pasting the stamps in her book, then closed it when she was done. There was a cold silence in the air, because I didn't know what to say to her, and I felt sad that she would say something so mean about my friend. I never looked at her the same way after that, because it felt odd to me, to love and respect someone, who could say something so cruel about my friend. She was raised in Tennessee during the depression and was taught very racist values at home. By her report, she never even saw anyone with skin color darker than hers, when she was a child.

Kids often repeat things innocently, not understanding what they mean. I knew not to repeat what my grandmother said, because I didn't like the way it sounded. The following day at school, I still played with my friend, and ignored my grandmother's words. She didn't change the way I looked at my friend, but she changed the way I looked at her. I had never seen, what I thought was, the mean side of her before. I knew that I could never talk to her about my friends at school again. The wrinkled nose and the scolding tone of her voice lingered with me. On the way home from school a few days later, my friends and I noticed that the turtle had been mutilated and stretched out across a small area of the sidewalk. I knew that if my friend had not put the turtle down, it would have been spared that gruesome fate. I wondered who could be so cruel as to do that. I was just starting to learn that there are a lot of things in life that are cruel, and that I wouldn't understand them until I grew up. I wouldn't understand a lot about my grandmother until I was grown up either. I always thought that being raised during the depression was what made her so stoic and thrifty with her money. No one could ever say that she wasn't willing to work hard, because it seemed as though she worked very hard her entire life, with no help from anyone. I couldn't understand what made her bitter about men, or about anyone who had skin that was darker than hers. She was not tolerant of difference outside of herself, or her comfort zone. When I questioned her about my mother's father, she recited what seemed like a well-rehearsed story of a handsome red headed soldier who slipped her a mickey and disappeared during the war. I had a feeling that really meant that she fell in love with him and he disappeared, leaving her to raise a child alone. Suffice it to say, I thought she coped with being lonely by occasionally glancing at the picture of Clark Gable on her nightstand, and watching Lawrence Welk on television. Most of her opinions and perceptions were shaped by what she saw in publications and on television. It was a good thing that I had my grandmother in Pennsylvania to moderate my values.

The Adventures of Markleberry Finn

Dad loved driving my brother and me, from Chicago all the way to the Appalachian mountain region of Pennsylvania on the turnpike, to visit Grandma and Grandpa Markle, every summer. Normally, long drives could be boring for kids, but Dad made it fun, by giving us a quarter for every out-of-state license plate we saw. It was actually quite smart of him to keep us from complaining about being bored, by having us count license plates.

By the time we made it to Pennsylvania, we had plenty of spending money for the summer, and that was often spent on things like sweet treats and toys that we shared with other kids in the neighborhood. In 1972 my parents began displaying symptoms of an unhealthy marriage. Neither of them seemed to be happy, and disagreements were becoming more frequent, amidst shoes flying. That summer was a huge relief from what seemed like geo-thermal pressure building between them. Dumping us at our grandparents' house would give them time to work things out or divorce.

The mountains and rivers of Pennsylvania provided the perfect solace from the stress of a lurking divorce. Grandma Markle was like a saint, who spent the entire summer teaching us how to fish, can vegetables and fruit, and sharing her virtuous life lessons with us. These were things most kids in big cities didn't get to experience, and I cherished that simple and most meaningful time with her.

Grandma Markle didn't have much money, but what she did have, she shared with us and even many of the other neighborhood kids. She prided herself on making gifts and baked goods for everyone. I valued those gifts the most because they were sentimental. It seemed easy to go to the store and buy a gift, but not as easy to make someone something, and that she put time and sentiment into her gifts, made them very special to me.

Several days during the week Grandma worked at a retail store by the name of J.J. Newberry's, which was in the town square next to the Juniata River. At the end of the day, she would take a long walk up the coal scattered alleys and side streets, carrying a bag of toys and treats for the neighborhood kids as prizes for playing Bingo. As I sat on the back porch swing, I watched her walk uphill in the heat of the sun, and I knew it was hard on her, yet she never complained. She made sure that even non-winners in the games got prizes, so that no one felt left out. This typified her generosity and spirit.

She had a moderate collection of Avon Products, and made it a point to look her best, both simply, and inexpensively. She had perfectly peachy skin, and only wore lipstick occasionally to appeal to Gordon, who seemed oblivious to her attempts to please him. His eyes generally stayed fixated on his baseball games.

Grandpa was an avid fisherman, cigar smoker, and couch potato. He was either lying around smoking cigars most days, or hiding up in the bedroom. It bothered me that he spent so much time ignoring my grandmother, and it made me curious as to why.

One morning when our grandmother was hanging laundry on the clothesline and Grandpa was fishing, I went upstairs, and decided to have a peek around in their room. I loved old humpback steamer trunks, and there was one in their bedroom, on my grandfather's side of the bed. I opened it, and what I saw made me realize why my grandmother was avoiding interacting with my grandfather as much as possible.

Although they said they are happy, I could tell they were not, and the reason was in the trunk. The junk in the trunk was why Gordon spent a lot of his free time upstairs. He was looking at nude magazines like *Playboy* and other swanky publications. The trunk was not locked, so she must've known they were there. I just couldn't understand why she was so complacent about it. I wondered why a man would need to look at another naked woman when he is married. Although I felt like Sherlock Holmes, the discovery also made me resent my grandfather. I thought it was rude that he would behave like that, and at the same time, have my grandmother wait on him. I didn't want to cause problems between them, so I just said nothing, until I could discuss it with her privately, someday.

Although Grandpa was not very kind to our grandmother, she never raised her voice to him, and politely accommodated him. Everything she did, she did graciously for the benefit of family, and unfortunately, that often included putting up with less than favorable days with Gordon, rather than stirring the mud, and speaking out about it. It wasn't until many years later that I understood what a womanizer was. In his mind, a woman's place was in the kitchen, waiting on him. Luckily for him, my grandmother loved being in the kitchen.

The back porch was behind the kitchen and had a fishing workbench or counter that was as long as the entire backside of the house. I could always tell what was for supper, because scattered atop that counter, there was usually at least one open tackle box, some fillet knives, miscellaneous scattered fish guts, and at the end of the line there was a small pile of tails.

I enjoyed playing in the river so much that it was difficult to get me out of it. I likened our experiences to *The Adventures of Huckleberry Finn,* because our days were spent carelessly daydreaming along the river, catching catfish, tadpoles, and unfortunately, Poison Ivy. It was a great place for our legs and our imaginations to run wild, without worrying about stranger danger. We were unattended all day long, and it was relatively safe back then.

Grandma Markle got up very early in the morning, to make sure that the kitchen table was laden with a wide variety of foods. Pancakes, eggs, and fresh blueberries with fresh cream and sugar on top of them were my favorites. After breakfast, we would help her clean the table and do the dishes. Before we set out to start the day, she would say, "You kids, have fun, watch out for Copperheads, and be back by supper!" We loved hearing that we would have no supervision until it was almost dark outside. With her well wishes, and words of caution in mind, we would spend the entire day swinging on monkey vines in the woods, hiking and swimming. Never once did we think about Chicago or about big city issues. Newport was a very racially homogenous community, but we never thought about it, as kids.

In Newport, I never heard anyone make a derogatory remark about anyone who was not Caucasian. Race was a subject that just didn't come up. My grandmother and grandfather would open their hearts and their doors to everyone. Many of the people in the community attended church, and everyone I met at church was very nice. Inadvertently, I came to assume that people who go to church do not say mean things, about anybody. Grandma went to church, but our grandfather did not. I thought it was because he felt guilty about the junk in his trunk.

The refrigerator was always well stocked with fresh milk that was bottled, my grandmother's cooking and canning, and a variety of treats from the Pennsylvania Dutch Amish farms. Because I was so fascinated by other cultures, I studied the lifestyle and artwork of the Pennsylvania Dutch (German). When we visited Lancaster, we made it a point to pick up their baked goods, peanut butter, dairy products, and some of their handmade arts and crafts. I also learned a few Pennsylvania Dutch words, which were basically German.

Gettysburg was a great place to learn a bit about the Civil War in the United States. As we were walking through the woods adjacent to the battleground, we had no idea that Dad walked there in advance of us, and secretly planted historical artifacts; such as old bullets, pieces from soldiers' boots, and uniform buttons. I was erroneously proud of myself for finding the artifacts. It took me years to figure out what Dad was laughing about, as I was high-fiving myself.

I could've been disappointed that I did not authentically find those things, but it was heartwarming to know that Dad would go to the extent that he did, to boost the experience. I had heard stories about the tragedies on battlefields, but I really didn't understand it until I held some of the soldier's artifacts in my hands. I realized that Dad's purpose for planting the artifacts and allowing us to find them, was so that maybe we could feel empathy about so many who lost their lives in war, rather than it just being about a tourist attraction. Although my father could fish, I usually went with my grandmother. She had the patience of a saint, and with my lack of fishing skills, that was a good thing. I never forgot the day first she took me fishing, and I caught her, instead of a fish. We hiked quite a distance through bushes to get to a clearing that opened up under beautiful moss overgrown, red brick railroad bridge. We walked around the stagnant pool, under the bridge and towards the river. When we got to our fishing spot, we set the fishing gear down on some rocks, under a large shady tree. I was exhausted by the time we got there, and it was a rather hot day, and the constant glare of the sun was almost blinding. Grandma picked up the end of my fishing pole, pulled the end of the fishing line to create some slack, and asked me to hold the rod. She walked a few feet away, and the sun was too bright to see if there was any slack in the line. Without knowing that she was putting bait on the hook, and had it in between her fingers, I pulled back on my pole, which thrust the fish hook deeply into her finger.

I looked at her face, and she was as calm as could be, but I let out a scream, comparable to something one might hear in a B rated horror movie. Very softly she said, "Don't worry, it's only a little hook". I knew it was painful, and that she was being calm so that I wouldn't feel bad about pulling on my line, which forced the hook into her finger. That's the kind of woman she was. She took a lot more hardship on herself, even pain, so that the rest of the family could have it easier. She loved with all that she was, and with all that she had, and then some. It was always sad to leave Newport at the end of the Summer to go back to Chicago. When it came time to say goodbye, I could always see Grandma was a bit teary-eyed, but she tried to cover it up by smiling and saying, "We'll see you next summer, and you do good in school. School is really important, because it's the one thing no one can ever take away from you, and you can always get a good job with it." Grandma's advice always lingered with me, and I couldn't help but wonder what had been taken away from her in her life, that made her say that. In retrospect, I think it was also due to the fact that during the depression, she had to be a family woman. Many women couldn't generally take jobs, because it was a man's world and she had kids. She once confided in me that, she worried that any day our Grandfather could walk out, and she would have nothing.

When I saw my grandfather's magazines in the trunk, I could understand why she might feel insecure. So, for her own false sense of security, and for the overall security of the kids, she learned to be stoic and diplomatic. She would never con- sider divorce as an option. Grandma Markle didn't get an education that would facilitate her getting a high-paying job.

I could see generational similarities between her and Grandma Loveless, especially their personal experiences with gender specific limitations, and economic strains coming out of the depression. When men went to war, women who were not parents, often went to work in factories such as the famous Rosie The Riveter. Gender equality was not a hot political topic, and for many women, it was a taboo subject that woman wouldn't really be more open about until the 1970's. Observing her struggles and challenges and sorrows was catalytic in my decision that I would always speak out when I felt something was unjust, and tell the truth, even if it made me unpopular.

CHAPTER FIVE

Change is the Only Constant

When we got back to Chicago, the argument and events leading up to my mother and father's divorce were like white noise. I became used to it. I was too young to hear the whole conversations and understand what caused the conflicts. I only remember standing in the hallway, as my mother was screaming at my father while he was in the shower. I didn't see it, but he allegedly got out, and slammed the door, not knowing that her middle finger was in the way. My mother was quite an animated screamer, so I had an idea about why her middle finger was up in the doorway. Something had to change, and I could sense that divorce was imminent.

As the '70s got into full swing, free love, rock and roll, and disco were social outlets for political tension and rebellion that arose out of the Vietnam war. Wild parties were everywhere, and they offered young Mod adults a wide array of tempting festivities, that contributed to my mother's resentment over being at home. She only had a high school education, and back in the 1950s, people were not taught how to be parents in school, and they knew nothing of child development. Most of what they learned, they learned from their parents, and their parents before them. Many schools taught home economics classes, but that's the least significant part of being a parent.

My mother often worked as a secretary and also at bartending jobs. After she and my father divorced, my dad frequently mentioned having given my mother child support that she never spent on us, so I assumed it was going to partying with grungy hippy friends. Her frustration and aggression escalated, and so did the partying. One would think her frustration would be alleviated, under the circumstances.

One Sunday, when my mother was having private time with one of her male acquaintances, my brother and I had spent the weekend with our father going to a fantastic Air and Water Show over Lake Michigan. That day was a slap in the face of reality. As we made our way through the crowd, we noticed my mother laughing and carrying on with her friend. He was a cheesy Walter Middy type, who lived vicariously through big time horse gamblers, and wore pastel polyester leisure suits, that made him look like an Easter egg, wearing slacks and sunglasses.

The day was almost over, and it would've been time for my father to take us home soon anyway, but he was suggesting that my mother and her boyfriend take us back to the apartment. She would have no part of her romantic day being interrupted by us, so she refused, and told my father that he would have to bring us to the apartment later.

Although she could have taken us home with her, she wanted a few more hours alone with the horse's ass whisperer. Dad ended up keeping us for a few more hours at the show, and then he took us home. The day ended on a good note in that it was clear that Dad would gladly spend more time with us. I dreaded going home with her.

For all of Grandma Loveless' idiosyncrasies and racist attitudes, she was very protective of my brother and me. My mother made a practice of using wooden household utensils as spanking devices, and my grandmother refused to allow it to continue. Between work and my mother's nightlife and dating, we spent more time with babysitters who were incompetent at caring for children. My only stability and solace was my father and my grandmothers, who compensated for what my mother lacked.

Luckily for me, my grandmother came over to the house one day, and like a tornado, she went through every cabinet and drawer, removing anything that could be used to hit us. Even though she was raised in Tennessee, and her parents spanked her with switches from apple trees, she did not believe in spanking. I had an unusual habit of raising my left eyebrow when I was curious about something. My mother would often look at me in a state of disgust, and say, "Stop doing that, you look just like your father." "Like father, like daughter," as the old saying goes.

Dad suggested that we live with him, which was like divine intervention. He found a great apartment near television studio. The schools were known to be good in that area, and we didn't hear from Dad. I felt like the situation was hopeless. I didn't know if he didn't call, or if my mother just wasn't giving me the messages. One day I got call from him, and as I was crying, I explained to him what was going on, and that I was terribly unhappy. Within a couple of days, I was on an airplane to Los Angeles, California. Dad picked me up at LAX Airport, and I was so happy that I cried when the plane landed. I was hopeful that we would finally have a chance of being a normal family. At that point in my childhood, I wanted a cheesy family scenario like that in the Brady Bunch, which portrayed a conservative and structured all-American middle-class blended family in the 1970s.

It was a hot smoggy day at LAX, but still it was the most beautiful sunny place I had ever seen. When I got off the plane, Dad was at the gate waiting for me. I ran over to him, and was so happy, I cried. He gave me a comforting hug and said, "I promised you that I would bring you out here when I got a job and an apartment. I just didn't get hired in television right away. I had to work as a hotel desk clerk for a while, and I was too ashamed to tell you". I felt sad that he would feel too embarrassed to tell me that he wasn't working at a studio yet. Even though I hadn't been away from him very long, it was a bit awkward reuniting. We had both changed a little bit, and I knew that there would be a period of reacquainting. A long moment of silence ended when we found his car in the parking garage. It was a modest, clean, gold Volvo. He opened the back passenger door, and put my luggage inside. I climbed into the front passenger seat. He got in, and we drove home. Although the car was only a modest Volvo, it felt like a chariot to me

.

CHAPTER SIX

Home Is Where the Heart Is

As we pulled closer to the building, I wanted to close my eyes and only open them when we stopped, so that it felt like a surprise. I squeezed them closed as tightly as I could, until I heard Dad say, "We are here." When I opened my eyes, I was in disbelief over finally seeing my new home.

Our apartment building was a basic, sand colored, three story apartment building, on the corner of Second and Idaho, in Santa Monica, but it was as grandiose as the Emerald City in *The Wizard of Oz* to me. As we pulled into the underground parking garage, I could see the Santa Monica Bluff, and part of the coastline to my left.

Once inside, we took an elevator to the third floor. The apartments were all situated around a very large, tropical garden courtyard. I looked around wondering if there were any kids who lived in the building, but the whole apartment complex was very quiet that day, without a soul in sight. We took the elevator up to the third floor, and then exited to Dad's apartment, which was a few doors to the left.

Because I always thought that decorating a home was a woman's forte, I was surprised at how spacious and tastefully decorated his apartment was. It was decorated in earth tones with generously spaced modern art. I was really happy to see that it wasn't a man cave, filled with dirty socks and other clutter. It felt very posh.

Dad dropped my bags down in the small room, that was off to the right of the sunken living room. That room that was once Dad's makeshift office, and it became my bedroom. I was so exhausted from the flight and drive, but I was overjoyed at being with Dad and anxious to hear about his job. All of his years of hard work at WTTW had paid off, and he got a well-paying job as a lighting director, on the daytime soap opera, *General Hospital*.

In a nerdy teenage squeal, I began listing all of the teenage actors that I wanted to meet at the studios. Southern California was swimming in celebrities, glamour, and money, which was a bit intimidating for a teenage girl like me, who had never picked up a teen fashion magazine. I had no idea how I could blend in with teenage girls who looked as though they jumped off the pages of *Seventeen* magazine. I knew I would have to study stacks of teen magazines to get ideas about how I would transform myself into a socially viable teen age girl. The walls of my bedroom soon became covered by pages torn out of *Tiger Beat* magazine, and other posters. I flipped through every magazine trying to find beauty tips and make up techniques that would work for me. Little did I realize at the time, that no matter what I did, there was no way that I would look like Farrah Fawcett. One day, I saw an advertisement for John Robert Powers Modeling School in Beverly Hills. I figured at a minimal, that I could learn to walk with books on my head, and develop some grace, but more than anything, I could learn how to apply make-up.

Twice a week, I rode the public bus up Wilshire Boulevard, from Santa Monica to Beverly Hills, to my classes. When I stepped off the bus, I was right in front of Neiman Marcus. Tourists driving by got a view of the prestigious and glamorous stores on Wilshire Boulevard, such as Neiman Marcus, and Saks Fifth Avenue, but, to their misfortune, they also got a glimpse of me. Traffic was at a standstill, and I thought that everybody was watching me walk clumsily in my wedged heel shoes. Just then, a large gust of wind rushed up the street, and it seemed to pick me as its clumsy dance partner. It circled around me, lifting my skirt completely above my head and arms, revealing my *Fruit of The Loom* underwear, that had brightly colored fruit bowl designs on them, and that were probably visible from a block away. I must've been six shades of red. To make matters worse, I twisted my ankle three times, getting from the bus stop to the classroom, so I was afraid to take another step in my rubber heels. I sat glumly, with my head resting on my hands during class, hoping to God that nobody sitting still in traffic, would ever recognize me. After a series of tragic comedies, I learned to walk somewhat gracefully, and apply make-up subtly enough that I could pass for looking human. Our instructor was a very sophisticated woman in her late '20s. The other students in the classroom were, like I was, awkward teenagers who just sat and stared at the beautiful woman whom we could never look like. She had long, silky, strawberry blonde hair, that she wore loosely clipped up in a bun, emerald green eyes, perfect lips, stark white teeth, and she was at least 5 foot 10.

When she walked in high heels on the miniature runway in the classroom, her clothing seemed to flow like a feather on a wind shear. When we tried to walk in heels at first, the fabric of our dresses, tangled in between our shoes, wrapped around our ankles. She must have developed such a great sense of humor from watching us. Without knowing it, we were giving back to her, for what she gave us. It was an interesting win-win situation. People have no idea what many young women go through just to fit in.

Within a couple of months, I had to scoot my Eric Estrada and Scott Baio posters over, to make room for Tom's Farrah Fawcett posters. I think Farrah Fawcett would have been mortified to know that millions of prepubescent boys, had experienced their first hormonal surges, as a result of looking at her posters. Although I carried picket signs around the apartment for several days, my brother Tom left Albuquerque, and came to live with us. Then this tiny office, that was the bedroom that I shared with my brother, would never be home to my pajama parties, unless I wanted my friends exposed to my brother's fart sounds, and rubber bands catapulted at the walls while we tried to have girl talk. I felt like my social life was doomed. I really wished then that I had a sister, because at least then I could still have sleepovers with my friends, and she would probably be a lot of fun.

Instead, I would be sleeping in a house of horrors, crowded by skateboards, dirty socks, and *Hot Rod Magazine* tear outs, taped to the wall. The family scenario was feeling complete, but there was one player missing. We needed a strong, nurturing, perfect step-mom. I could only imagine how my father felt, realizing he had two teenage kids on his hands who needed a mother figure also, and that he would have to wear a lot of hats until and unless he remarried.

Carolyn stayed in Chicago and, although I was hoping she would come to Southern California, that didn't happen. I didn't really think my dad would meet anybody who was intellectual or creative quickly, and he wasn't the type to date bimbos, even though my mother was gregarious and very physical. He seemed like he had become much shyer as he got older. Conversely, I knew he would definitely never pair up with a conservative Betty Crocker type of woman either. Grandma Markle was somewhat of a Betty Crocker type, but I doubted that he would marry someone like his mother. Although some men do that, I always thought it was a bit creepy. As much as I idealized the perfect step- mom, I also knew that she had to be someone that made Dad happy and I was really open to whomever he chose to be with.

CHAPTER SEVEN

Auditioning Mom's

Since my dad very eclectic taste in women, I was exposed to a wide variety of cultures and cuisine. One of my favorite girlfriends of his, was a lovely woman from Thailand, who I remember as Gail, who lived an hour away from us, and had a son who was close to my age. She was very hospitable, smiled genuinely, was family oriented, and always cooked the most amazing food. She really enjoyed teaching us Thai words, and as much as she could about the food. I believed then, and I still believe that for most kids, and for many people, one of the most wonderful things about any culture is the food. I hoped that Dad would marry Gail, but some reason they stopped seeing each other. It must've been a lot of pressure on women who dated my Dad, to discover that they had to impress two young teenage kids, and pass whatever test criteria had been put in place by us. It probably would have stressed them out to know the reality was, that when they visited, or when they made us dinner, they were really auditioning for the role of stepmom. Realistically, that woman would have to fit our lives in order to be an integral part of our family. The audition for our potential stepmom, always took place in the kitchen. I had heard that in Hollywood there was something known as the casting couch. In our house it was the casting stove. We liked good food, and we certainly wanted a stepmom who could cook.

I was glad that my brother Tom moved in with us, but room we shared, started to feel really small. I was almost 14, he was 13. Neither of us had privacy, so we took turns dressing, which made it feel like bedroom time share living. Outside activities broke up some of the monotony of feeling crowded together in the apartment. We both went to the Junior High School that was only a few blocks away from the apartment building, and we made an average amount of friends.

I didn't blend in with the blonde, suntanned surfer girls, so I found my comfort zone with the smart, geeky kids, who hung out around the drama department. We were all a bit awkward, so I felt like I blended in there without much effort. Out- side of our immediate neighborhood, there was so much to do between home and Hollywood. Dad regularly took me with him to Sunset Gower Studios in Hollywood, and much of my time there was spent unsupervised. My favorite memory, involved one of his productions meeting at Paramount Studios. When we arrived there, he said,"Get lost and just have fun until I'm done with my meeting", which was my cue to go climb scaffoldings, and confiscate snacks from the green rooms. I wandered around the hallways, the control booths, and climbed up and walked across catwalks, while fantasizing that I owned the sound stages. I had always done whatever I wanted to do at WTTW in Chicago, so I felt comfortable wandering every- where I could. I often curious cat on the scaffoldings. I never considered that studio security personnel, probably didn't like it, because of the possibility of injury liability for the studios.

As part of my self-directed tour, I strolled onto the set of, *All in The Family*, and ended up sitting in the production booth. Carol O'Conner was the brilliant actor, who portrayed the character of *Archie Bunker*. I knew the show was about a 1970's family adjusting to changing social and political norms, including interracial marriage. The show's character Archie, was bigoted, and a stereotypical bigot. It was a shockingly hilarious, and to some, perhaps an offensive situation comedy, that contrasted Archie's rigid, ignorant values, with radically changing social values and norms.

Because I had watched the show periodically, I had always imagined the actor to be a mean old coot in person. I had formed a stereotype of the men that his character represented. Contrary to that stereotype, I was surprised to find that Mr. O'Conner was kind, gentle, and completely the opposite of his character.

Although television shows are fictional, they still send social messages about people. I was only a kid but I thought about that quite a bit. After I left that set, I explored the set of Hermann Wouke's *Winds of War*. I sat out of sight on the side of the set, watching divers and crew, set up mini ships, in a large pool of water, that was placed in front of a giant backdrop that had ominous thunder clouds painted on it. I was so fascinated at what went into making a movie. I was in awe of what my father did, and how productions came together. I decided then, that I wanted to work in some capacity behind the camera. I also realized how difficult and technical production is, compared to how easy it looks on the screen. Holly- wood makes everything look easy and glamorous. One of the first tours of Hollywood Dad gave me, was to show me that Hollywood itself, is anything but glamorous.

We drove along Hollywood Boulevard, and instead of doing the typical tour that included Grauman's Chinese Theatre, Dad pointed out the run down condemnable apartments, above the businesses on Hollywood Boulevard. Many of which were filled with life stories of people who moved to Hollywood to get their big break , and ended up broke and unknown.

Sadly, some of those apartments were home to well-known actors from days gone by, who drank themselves into obscurity, and poverty, when their fairy tale ended.

If I wanted to learn anything about Hollywood, Dad was the go to guy. Although he worked in television, and was of- ten invited to nightlife festivities, he wasn't the party type. He was very serious about work, and spent his free time with us, often including us in his daily adventures. I don't remember him ever going out on dates at night. He never put his roman- tic and social life ahead of us, but rather he included us, and scheduled his personal time appropriately.

Dad was generally comfortable being without a romantic partner, but I thought that he needed a great woman who could complement his life, in ways that my mother never did. I couldn't imagine who he would meet that would fit my unrealistic expectations.

CHAPTER EIGHT

Smooth Operator

After long awaited anticipation, he introduced us to the woman that he had been seeing casually for a couple of weeks. She worked for a temp agency and was hired to fill in as a secretary. I guess Dad got all of the memos she sent in his direction.

Doria seemed sweet and schoolgirl-like. She had short dark curly hair, that always looked perfect. She was only 21, but she seemed quite mature for her age. She was very well-dressed, and naturally pretty, with a medium golden complexion. She always smelled like Halston perfume. She had a great smile, but I had heard somewhere that if a person smiles all of the time, be wary.

She definitely didn't need to hide anything behind makeup, because she had a natural beauty, and used lip balm, and moisturizer with a light dusting of bronze mineral powder known as Indian Earth. She was also taking classes in makeup artistry, and had a large supply of make-up, but it was for professional use only. I enjoyed looking at the stick make-up for actors, because there were so many tubes of different and subtle tones, and a good make-up artist could match them to anyone's skin precisely.

I admired her upscale, casual taste in clothing. She had a good figure, and often wore beautifully textured and patterned, wrap around skirts, that never looked as good on me as they did on her. I thought that I had a figure like a pear on stilts. She was petite, and a size 6. Because she was so young, she seemed more like she was my older sister or a peer, than a potential step-mom. I was pleasantly surprised that she was simple, and natural. She seemed to have a very matter-of-fact way about her, that I think was calming for Dad, at least in the beginning.

Because I had completed modeling school, A.K.A, The Homely Teenager Transformation Institute, I was eager to look through Doria's make-up kit and books. She shared some of her techniques with me, and I was most fascinated by some of the tutorials on how to apply old age make-up.

Doria seemed to enjoy being around us, and we liked her. It wasn't long before she moved into Dad's bedroom. It was kind of strange at first, but we were all somewhat easy-going, and it was nice to have company and laughter in the apartment.

I had completed part of the school year at Santa Monica High School. I loved it there, but still I didn't feel like I fit in with the surfer girls, even though I had grown a bit, and could apply lip gloss correctly (in the lines), it was still a really tough teenage year.

The living together situation seemed great at first, but the apartment soon felt like a hamster cage. Dad and Doria made periodic romantic weekend getaways to Santa Barbara. I should've known that something was brewing in terms of a wedding, because during the previous month, I had spent a couple of mornings in Hollywood with Dad, at an odd little place, that I thought was a hippie church. It was The Self Realization Fellowship Temple on Sunset Boulevard.

I was very naïve about religions. I thought the building was a Hari Krishna temple or something. I had seen the Hari Krishna dancers in town, or at the airport dancing around in the white toga-like garments, shaking tambourines. I expected them to pop out from behind a building at any time with their tambourines, but they didn't. We walked around the property, and I thought that it seemed more like an office building courtyard, than a church. I thought at first that Dad was looking at it to do a remote shoot for *General Hospital* or something else for television. When he told me, it was to be the home of his wedding, I was surprised, but it was up to them where they felt most comfortable getting married.

My second semester of High School was ending for me in a few months. Santa Monica High School was, in my mind, a typical beach community high school, with a handful of celebrities attending. It was a great experience for me as a teenager, to see that people are seldom as they are perceived in the media. It was my teenage awakening to the fact that celebrities are just people. Being in Southern California around so much glamour, and so much money, made me appreciate the small things in life, and I quickly became bored of all that glitters.

Dad was not very sensationalistic. He was happy with a simple life, and even in Hollywood, he worked very hard just to have solitude. It soon made sense to me that so many people in Los Angeles work so much, just to be able to retreat and have a quiet simple life and family time. More than anything, I wanted a family that would all sit down at the dinner table at the same time, have family outings and grow old together, often laughing about days gone by. I got home from school one afternoon, set my backpack down in my bedroom, and walked into the sunken living room.

Tom strolled in, and we both noticed that Dad and Doria had pie eating grins on their faces. I looked curiously at them, as Dad said, "Come sit down, we have some exciting news. We're getting married!" That was great news, but they weren't done. "We need a bigger house, and Doria found us one," Dad added. Although I was pleasantly surprised about everything, I felt that my brother and I should've had some say in picking the house. "Is it by the beach?!" I asked. "No, it's in Woodland Hills, in the Valley. It's a 3-level house, and it's really cute," Doria chimed in. I was relieved at the idea of having a bigger house, and in a relatively conservative neighborhood. The following day, we made the trip to 21836 Providence Dr. It was a quiet, middle class cul-de-sac street that was about to come up a few hundred decibels.

The streets in the neighborhood were lined with Eucalyptus trees that reminded me of Weeping Willow trees. When we pulled up in front of the house, we jumped out of the car, and ran to the front door. Immediately to the left, just inside the door, was a very large living room complete with the fireplace, and a large window, adjacent to a very large dining room.

The kitchen was as wide as the entire back of the house. Pretty blue Mediterranean linoleum tile covered the floors all the way through the kitchen, wrapping back around to the front foyer. The kitchen was home to a very large pantry and laundry room, that was hidden behind long folding doors. The bottom floor was home to the recreation room that was quite large, and the door that led to the interior of the garage.

The top level of the house had two bedrooms on the right at the top of the stairs, a bathroom down in the center of the hallway to the left, followed by what would be my bedroom on the very left, and my brother's bedroom was directly across the hall from my room, on the right. My bedroom and Tom's were situated over the backyard patio.

The architect of the house must have had kids and known that having the kids' bedrooms over the patio would spare people below from noise generated by teenage stampeding feet. At the bottom of the stairs, just to the right was a small office and then, set behind that, was Dad and Doria's bedroom, which was on the right side above the garage. Their bedroom was quite large, it had a moderately sized closet and on the other side of the closet, was their own private bathroom.

Although the backyard was not very large, the house was so big, it didn't matter to us. I was happy we were moving there. I would miss the beach, but I could say goodbye to Santa Monica. Ocean access was a matter of a quick 15minute drive through Topanga Canyon, which had its own beachy, hippy shops, and restaurants. Although the area of Woodland Hills, such as the South of Ventura Boulevard area, is notable for upscale stores, and progressive development, Topanga Canyon seemed to be stuck in the 70's.

Moving into the house was a lot of fun. I decorated my bedroom in blue and white delicate flowers. 1979 would be the first time that I had a real bedroom, unlike the office crash pad in Dad's apartment in Santa Monica. My closet was somewhat small, and the opening to the attic was on the ceiling inside of it. I didn't have a large wardrobe, and what I did have would mostly fit in my drawers, so it wasn't an issue, at first anyway.

Tragically, right across the hall from me, was my brother's bedroom, that I was convinced was going to be the home to any number of missing neighborhood animals. The first week there was of course spent doing typical organizing and unpacking of boxes. The smooth operator had everything under control. I was trying to be easy going and appreciative, but there was that initial awkwardness of having a newcomer in the family, somewhat controlling how things went in the house. At first, being in the house together was awkward, because we didn't want to step on each other's toes, and we were still at the polite stage of being a new family.

I knew that my brother loved the house, because it had a large recreation room downstairs, where he could hang out with his friends, and the cul-de-sac street was perfect for skateboarding. I was hoping that we would have a swimming pool, but the backyard was entirely too small. Nonetheless it was perfectly shady and breezy. I think we might've gotten bored of the swimming pool within a matter of weeks, anyway, because we would rather be running around the neighborhood, and going to the beach.

I never paid attention to the racial or ethnic composition in our neighborhood because it didn't matter, and I didn't think anything would be different than it was when we were kids in Chicago. I did notice that most of the people in the neighborhood seemed like they had a lot of money, as evidenced by three-bedroom homes and perfectly manicured lawns. Most of the driveways had sports cars and luxury cars parked in them, so I just assumed that we lived in an upper middle-class neighborhood. Compared to what I had seen in Chicago, I thought it was moderately wealthy.

CHAPTER NINE

The Shady Bunch of Woodland Hills

Dad and Doria got married on December 23rd of 1979. Doria was only 22, Dad was 37. As a wedding dress, Doria wore a pretty white cotton schoolgirl style dress, with short sleeves, and a ring of baby's breath around her short curly black hair. Dad was very sweet and nervous, and looked humbly handsome in his herringbone jacket and tie. I remember looking at Dad and Doria and giggling at how much in love they looked, but it was almost like a high school crush kind of love. I was open to getting to know Doria, as more of a family member than when she seemed to be when she was just living with us in Santa Monica. In attendance at the wedding were me, my brother Tom, Doria's mother Jeanette, and Father Alvin, Doria's sister Sandy. Sandy was very conservative and professional looking. She had a golden complexion, with a delicate sprinkle of freckles across her nose, and she fit right in because we all had freckles. Sandy's boyfriend Eugene, who reminded me of Lurch from *The Adams Family* and a couple of Doria's friends, Loren, Candy and Dad's friend Bee were all there. Loren had arctic blonde hair, bright ocean blue eyes, wore perfect make-up; overall, she quite was stylish.

Candy was tall and slender, had a dazzling smile, and beautiful model like features. They were always very cheerful and referred to me by my nickname Babe. Doria's friends and family referred to her as Dodi. Doria called Dad Bunky. I didn't mind being called Babe even though it seemed like a kid's name. If Babe Ruth didn't mind his nickname, I thought that I shouldn't mind mine.

After the wedding, the house was filled with excited reception guests, friends and family rushing in and out of the door, before and after the wedding. Dad's friend, Kay (name changed for privacy), really helped to make sure that the reception had everything that was needed. Kay worked in television and was very sophisticated. As I got to know her, I wished that Dad had married her, but they were only platonic friends.

Dad and Doria didn't go on a honeymoon and, the next day, life resumed as normal. I had to transfer from Santa Monica High School to Taft High School. Starting school in the middle of the year was awkward, because everyone else at school had already arranged themselves into cliques and groups, and I was the nerdy newcomer, who didn't know anyone. My Dad dropped me off at school in the morning, and the whole day seemed like a tornado of Louis Vuitton handbags and lip gloss, swirling past me in the hallways. With Christmas approaching, there was more of a jovial attitude in the hallways, and of course the normal banter about what everybody was going to get for Christmas; like new Jaguars or other pricey sports cars. I didn't want to look like a nervous newcomer, so I just smiled a lot. As I looked around, I knew one thing for certain. I needed new clothes to blend in. I didn't have a car yet, but I knew I wouldn't be getting a Jaguar. At the end of the day, I stood in front of the building, contemplating taking the bus home, when a spunky blonde girl, with a pixie like-face, who reminded me of Sandra Dee, approached me carrying a pair of skis. "Hey, ya need a ride home?" she asked. She was very smiley, considering that it was the end of the day. I told her where I lived, and in a burst of excitement, she said, "Wow, you only live a street away from me! Come on, I'll give you a ride!" I was relieved, and I thought that it was a very sweet gesture, on the part of my new friend. I had never met anyone who was so friendly. Nicole was so perfect in every way. She had silky blonde shoulder length hair, golden tan skin, large brown fun eyes, a very small button nose, and a gorgeous dazzling ear to ear smile, that was only punctuated by an insidious, rolling laugh. She was the kind of girl who looked like she should be snobby, but she was not. I had heard the term contagious laugh before, but I had never met anyone whose laugh could make me laugh. Some people tried to laugh like she did, and they ended up sounding like a woodpecker.

I was trying to fill air space with any conversation, so I thought I would try a compliment. "Cute car," I said. "I'm getting rid of it, and getting a convertible!" she proudly chimed. It was somewhat predictable that she was getting a new car. After she said that, it gave me the idea that maybe, I could buy her car. "How much would you sell this one for?" I asked. I was both excited and shocked when she said "Only $500." It was nothing fancy, but at least it ran. I wasn't the only teenager in Woodland Hills, who had to take the bus, but I had a mile to walk home from the bus stop, and I dreaded it at the end of the day. "Let me ask my Dad, and I will let you know," I replied. Nicole had a funny, and spunky way of over enunciating some words. She flipped her hair, looked over towards me and said, "Groovaaaaay." I had not heard the word groovy since I heard it in *The Brady Bunch*,

As we sped up Ventura Boulevard towards our houses, I fidgeted nervously with the zipper on my backpack. I knew that, at any moment, my carrot top, freckle-faced brother, would speed up on his testosterone powered skateboard. The last thing I wanted was my adolescent brother, lustfully salivating over my new friend. I think that most teenagers are apprehensive about having their friends meet family members, regardless of whether or not those concerns are legitimate. I knew that he would also want to spend at least 20 minutes, showing Nicole skateboard tricks, up and down the street.

Even though I had been to modeling school, I wore too much make-up when I wore it, but I thought it looked cool, even though it was bright enough to stop a speeding truck at midnight. *New Wave* was the trendy thing so the bright colors provided me with an excuse to wear a bit too much. I called myself trendy, instead of gaudy. Singers like Sheena Easton, and many others were starting to cut their hair shorter, an '80s style, at least in the music industry, and I really wanted something that was easy to manage, so I lopped it off at an overpriced Beverly Hills Salon. My brother Tom wasn't at the age where he was too worried about his hair, as he zipped around on a skateboard, thinking that he was the equivalent of Tony Alva. As Nicole and I turned and wound our way up Don Pio Drive, the sweeping branches of Eucalyptus trees seemed to sway to the beat of the Go-Go's, that was blasting out of the car windows. I thought that I was a cool nerd. I was sure that music was loud enough to rattle some of the neighbors' ear drums. I loved to sing, but my voice had a resonance and quality similar to that of a dog trying to bark while wearing a muzzle. Slowly we pulled up to the curb in front of the house and stopped. Just then, Nicole's eyes got as big as half dollars, and her nostrils flared it as if there were marbles stuffed in each one of them, when she screeched, "Who is that woman on your lawn, what is she smoking?" I was numb. " Uh, she's not smoking anything," I mumbled. Smoke drifted across the front of the lawn, and it smelled like marijuana, but I wouldn't admit that to Nicole. Our neighborhood was somewhat conservative and quiet, so I hurried to change the subject. "Oh that's my step-mom. She and my Dad just got married. She's kind of a casual type." I should have thought it was cool that my stepmother was a liberal, partying type, because theoretically that should've made me a popular kid in high school, with all my friends wanting to come over and hang out.

What came next was an uncomfortable surprise. She looked at me, oddly stating the obvious, "She's black." "So!" I replied. I thought the question was rude and very awkward but I didn't know that Nicole came from a very homogenous family.

I thought that racism ended, when the '70s ended. I was in Chicago as a child, and I knew that people all look different, and it was not an issue. For some it can be an uncomfortable subject. Because of my limited personal experiences, I really believed that racism didn't exist much anymore, and diversity was becoming the norm. I was only sixteen, and I thought I knew it all. The only person other than Nicole whom I had ever met who mentioned a person's skin color was Grandma Loveless. I remembered the horrible remark that she made to me when I was in first grade. It became the uncomfortable fact in the family, that my grandmother would have predictably racist responses, about anyone whose skin color was the slightest tone darker than hers was. I remember thinking as a kid that, "Grandma just needs a Black boyfriend."

I secretly hoped that she would open her heart and mind about people before she passed away, because she seemed lonely. I didn't feel ready to be confrontational with my friend, but I felt that she would have to get over whatever her issue was about skin color.

My stepmother had a medium olive skin, and I thought it was beautiful. I was not uncomfortable with our difference in skin color, I was uncomfortable seeing her smoking, and wearing a bathrobe in the front yard. Suffice it to say, that I was at that age where social referencing was normal, as I had an immature self-esteem, and was constantly concerned about others' opinions of me. Oddly, our next-door neighbors to the left of our house, a very conservative mother and her teenage daughter, never came out to say hello. I couldn't help but wonder if they smelled smoke drifting in their windows.

My idea about having the picture perfect family, and fun neighbors, was probably unrealistic. I was so preoccupied with what others thought about us, that I didn't stop to think that no one is perfect, and maybe the neighbors didn't say hello, because they were busy or socially shy. I knew there was plenty of time for getting acquainted with neighbors. I would've invited them over to our house, but we weren't completely settled in, and there were some things going on in my house that I wasn't ready to expose the neighbors to. One day, after I had just come inside the house, and climbed the hallway stairs, I noticed on the right side of the wall, there was an interesting picture that I had not seen before. Sitting on the railroad tracks in Santa Barbara, was a bare, bronze skinned, woman with her legs folded up in front of her. No private body parts were showing. In fact, it revealed much less than a picture of a woman in a bathing suit would. I looked closer at it and realized that it was a tasteful bare skinned photograph of Doria, taken by my father, but it was on the wall in our hallway! I knew I would take it down if any of my friends came to the house. I felt silly for being embarrassed by it though, because her body was fully shielded behind her arms and legs. Seeing the picture on the railroad tracks made me realize that Santa Barbara was their romantic hideaway. That was a little too much information for my teenage brain. I couldn't help but wonder how long it would be before we got the news that there would be Markle Baby Number Three on the way. I think I started running the clock from the moment I saw that picture on the wall. I knew what was up. Well, if the escapades in Santa Barbara didn't pave the way for Baby Number Three, there was always Christmas spirit looming to spark the mood. I was excited to hear that Grandma Markle would be making a trip out to see the new house sometime after Christmas! We were all excited to bring her to the new house, show her around Southern California, and let her see that all of her self-sacrifice was paying off, and that Dad and the rest of the family were doing really well, largely thanks to her. She lived in Florida, and every birthday or Christmas, she would still make rum balls, put them into tin cans, and send them to us along with other gifts and trinkets. Anything that Grandma made was cherished.

Doria had never met Grandma Markle, so it would be a fun gathering; we all were excited about it. I was sure that she would be inquisitive, just as she had before I was born, prodding and encouraging the production of another grandchild. She was getting up in years, and I knew that would be a joy for her.

Christmas Day was spent at Doria's mother, Jeanette's house. It was perfectly festive, and we could smell the cooking from outside the front door. Jeanette lived in Los Angeles, not too far from La Brea, in a quaint little apartment that I remember as a duplex. From the second she opened the door, she was smiling and had that red wine and Johnny Mathis twinkle in her eyes. She had baby soft skin, with a few freckles sprinkled across her nose and cheeks and, although she had had a hard life, she was welcoming, and kind. I often wanted to ask her about the hardships in her life, but it was not my business, and I didn't want to ruin her good mood, so I didn't ask. I remember commenting on the fact that "Johnny Mathis was really handsome and had a great voice." She just raised her eyebrows smiled and said, "*mmmmm hmmmm.*" I giggled to myself when she said that, because her tone of voice suggested a little romance and fun in her past. Jeanette was married to Doria's father, Alvin, and that they had been divorced for quite a few years. The twinkle in her eyes, and the tone of her voice, let me know loudly and clearly that Johnny Mathis was her dream man. Johnny Mathis' Christmas songs echoed sweetly through the house. The turkey was in the oven. Doria's sister Sandy and her boyfriend Eugene came over too. "Dodi, we just need the pies," Jeanette said. Dodi was Doria's nickname. "Can I go?" I asked excitedly. Doria grabbed her purse and keys, and with that, we both headed out to go get the sweet potato pies. I loved Southern comfort food, especially Creole food.

Doria was a good cook when it came to her specialties; one of them being Louisiana style seafood gumbo. She would make a giant pot of it, and put in every kind of seafood possible, but it was her seasoning that really made it. Everyone in the house had seconds, and there was seldom any leftover. Since the oven was full, it was quicker and easier to get the pies at Mama Kizzy's Kitchen. Dad was very chivalrous, and always put something under the tree from all of us. He never showed up at anyone's house without a nice bottle of wine and flowers, or at Christmas, a beautiful arrangement. Doria's Father's, Alvin, also came to holiday get-togethers. He was very kind and gentle. He was clean shaven, not very tall, had a medium build, wore round scholarly glasses, and was always dressed well. I thought that Doria looked more like him, than like her mother. Both were attractive, so it was easy to see where Doria got her good looks. Alvin had a wonderful and very large antique store in Los Angeles, and although it wasn't elaborate, it was stocked full of some very amazing pieces of furniture from the turn of the century. I had only been there a couple of times, but it was quite memorable. It was nice to experience our new family over the holidays. After meeting everyone, I got the sense that we would all blend together very well. By February of 1981, I had settled into a normal school schedule, and had taken a part-time job on the weekends at a little donut shop around the corner from our house. At Blinkie's Donuts, I earned extra money for things I wanted, that were over and above necessities. I was starting to think about saving money for a car. I had my eye on Nicole's car, but hadn't spoken with her about it again. I only made seven dollars an hour, but I also got tips for being the smiley cashier, who handed everybody a donut and a cup of coffee in the morning.

Greeting customers was the glamorous part of the job, and then there was the reality of scraping three inches of sugar off the floor near the fryers and prep tables. In addition to my cashier job, I also did a few small modeling jobs.

I wasn't really the model type yet and felt somewhat out of place around working models, but it made me a little extra money. I made some new friends, and I learned about photography and make-up. I had a feeling some of the photographers might be irritated by the fact that I was asking so many questions, while they were working. Since my dad was a lighting director, lighting was my favorite part of photography.

CHAPTER TEN

One World

I was fascinated by the traditions of other countries, and I had never met anyone from the Middle East, until I met one of my dearest friends Azitar at school, and instantly adored her.

Azita's mother was one of the most beautiful and famous women in Iran, and was treated as royalty in public, even in the United States. She was an actress and a belly dancer, and Azita's father was also very successful in Iran. I had never seen authentic belly dancing before meeting Azita's mother. It's not as easy as it looks. She could methodically move muscles in her body, that Grey's Anatomy didn't know existed. I was also privileged to meet other extraordinarily creative, and talented people in her social circle. Most notable was their hospitality, grace, and warmth. I really enjoyed the simplicity having tea with them, because it promoted conversation with family and friends, that we often miss in our busy lives.

By the time I was 15, I had eaten Mexican food, Spanish food, French food, Indian food, Thai food, Japanese food, Chinese food Armenian food, Greek food, Northern and southern Italian food, Cuban food, Peruvian food, and Jamaican food. I had never previously had the opportunity to try Persian food. I mused over the fact that people can be worlds apart, and come together at a dinner table.

Azita had a speedy, red, convertible Honda, and one day she was going to Westwood, and asked if I'd like to go. I took her up on the offer, and we went to a fantastic Persian restaurant. I wasn't familiar with many of the foods on the menu, so I let her order for me. I had eaten a wide variety of food at her house, but this menu was quite different. I sat at the table, while Azita stood in line to order for us. When she came back to the table with our plates, she set my food down, and I couldn't wait to taste it. I had eaten Saffron rice before, but there was something yellow and spongy on the plate beside it, that looked like scrambled eggs. I assumed that it was probably only eggs, so I didn't ask what it was. We both started eating, I took a bite of the yellow spongy substance, and it felt really unique in my mouth, but I was trying to be open-minded and polite. I said, "Oh this is different. What is it?" Azita looked at me and smiled, because she knew I was going to be shocked when she said, "Oh, that's lamb brain." Out of respect, I smiled, chewed, and swallowed it. I reminded myself of the fact that, what was considered normal meat in United States, like beef ribs, or chicken, or even pork, was also eating animals. I was not on a vegetarian diet at that time. I did not eat meat very much, but I tried to be open about it. I smiled cordially and said, "It's really different." I always believed that when we share someone's culture, it is rude to express dislike of food that is offered. I was grateful that she shared it with me. It tasted good, but it was the texture that was very different from any meat I had ever eaten. Overall, I felt like I had a fun new adventure, and definitely learned something about Middle Eastern food. I also wanted to be multilingual and was fortunate to learn a bit of Farsi, which is a beautiful language. My High School was culturally diverse, and as such, it was also one of the schools in Los Angeles that was taking part in desegregation and bussing. In an effort to give kids from underfunded schools in Central Los Angeles the opportunity to attend suburban schools that had more resources and therefore a higher quality of education, students were transported by busses to those schools, including mine. As I was putting my books in my locker one morning, I overheard a group of students walking through the hallway complaining about them coming to our school. I also heard, in passing, that many of the parents were not in favor of bussing, and were concerned about violence at the school, as a result of bringing kids who didn't have a lot of money, to our school where many kids and family lived on upwards of $200,000 a year.

I thought that all students should be given the opportunity to excel and compete in better schools, without feeling excluded. I didn't think it was fair that incoming students would be subjected to an environment that made them feel unwanted or inadequate. Without knowing details, within a couple of weeks, I had heard about fights in the parking lot, and I thought it was and hurtful to students who were coming in. I tried to imagine how I would feel if I was one of them. Because I was in a new interracial family, I was more aware of, and sensitive to the social tension surrounding desegregation and bussing. As much as I wanted to believe it was just about economic disparity, I had also heard rude remarks in the hallways, about skin color.

I stayed at my school, but my brother was being bussed from his Junior high school in Woodland Hills to an inner-city Los Angeles Junior high school. Tom had freckles and bright red hair, so my Dad and Doria as an interracial couple, were concerned that, it might not be a safe environment for my brother, because of the likelihood of his being picked on, for standing out like a sore thumb.

Tom did deal with some bullying, and although Dad and Doria went to the school, and expressed that they did not feel the need for him to have exposure to ethnically diverse backgrounds, because we were an interracial family, the school still said that he had to go to Audubon Junior High, as part of the bussing program. I had heard that, by late April, that parents would have the option of keeping their kids in the bussing program, or returning to schools near their homes. I didn't think it was fair that teenagers should be the litmus test of racial and socioeconomic integration.

It was unfair of the school district to haphazardly bring kids from poorer districts to a school where they felt relatively deprived. Prior to starting the bussing program, there should have been counselor interaction, and extensive discourse coupled with preparation, so that the kids would not be placed abruptly in a conflicted social environment that distracted them from learning, and forced them into unnecessary positions of self-defense, due to peer pressure, and socioeconomic strain.

We were all kids in the same city, and yet it felt like we were worlds apart, because of the unnecessary tension that was created. The bussing program seemed to have the opposite effect of its goal, in that it perpetuated animosity and stereotypes about both incoming students and students at the host schools. I thought it could have worked if the planning was more intensive, so that more students and parents embraced it, and felt comfortable with it. Kind and welcoming treatment of incoming students should have been mandated, and briefing on multi-cultural awareness should have occurred to make the transition a positive one.

It was really disappointing that a program that was designed to bring students from many walks of life together, didn't work because of poor planning and, as a result, many Los Angeles students did not benefit from the program. In late April, when parents had the option to continue bussing, or stay in schools in their own neighborhoods, my brother returned to his Junior High School.

I spent a lot of time trying to empathize with kids who feel marginalized because they were different either on the basis of skin color or socioeconomic status. Kids have a natural need to fit in, and I knew that because I felt the same way trying to fit in at my high school. The teen years are a very difficult time and school administrators should've been more sensitive to the social dynamics of students, before bussing them to schools out of district.

Flower Power

One afternoon in early May, as I climbed stairs in the hallway to go up to my bedroom, Doria raced past me with an arm full of clothing that were still wrapped in plastic and on hangers with tags on them. I moved out of her way, and watched as she pirou-etted across the room, and landed a stack of clothing perfectly on the bed, like a fanned out deck of cards. I looked at the tags on some of the garments, and they were not her normal size 6. They were a size 9, which was my size. Since some of them were larger, I could not help but wonder if they were for me, so I blurted out naively, "Oh, that was nice of you! You got me clothes, too." I picked up one of the skirts, and looked curiously at it, because it was my size. To my surprise and disappointment, she grabbed it out of my hand, and laid it back down on the bed.

There was a moment of uncomfortable silence and then, with an interesting Cheshire cat grin on her face, and a triumphant tone in her voice, she said, "I have a surprise, Babe!" Just then, she pointed a few feet away to something that I hadn't even noticed. There was a Jenny Linn swinging bassinet in the corner. I knew it wasn't for the cats to sleep in. "A baby?" I asked.

I sat down on the bed next to her, and she pulled up her shirt revealing her pregnant stomach, and said, "Here, let me have your hand, Babe." Then, she put my hand on her stomach, and I could feel something large and angular moving under her skin. "We are having a baby, Babe!" she said jubilantly. I felt that maybe she was attempting to bond with me in a way that we had not. I had never seen a pregnant stomach up close, except on PBS educational programs. I wondered if at any moment, like in the movie *Aliens* something would pop out of her stomach, and eat me alive, head first, leaving only my sneakers on the ground. I could tell that whoever the baby was in there, he or she, could make moves that only yoga masters and ballerinas could make. At that moment, all of my questions about the trip to Santa Barbara in the railroad tracks made sense. Markle Baby Number Three was on the way! I didn't know if it was a girl or boy but it dawned on me that, all of a sudden, my brother and I would have to become responsible as "big brother and sister." At the same time I panicked, because I knew that, as Doria got closer to delivering the baby, I would probably have to do most of the household chores because getting my brother to clean house would be like trying to suck apple juice out of a rock. I also knew that the squabbles that my brother and I had would have to stop, because it would startle the baby.

It was as if the clouds parted, and Doria suddenly seemed motherly, and I felt guilty for thinking about absconding with clothing out of her closet. What teenage girl has not borrowed her mother or stepmother's clothing out of the closet without asking? For some reason, I was taken aback that she was carrying a Markle baby in her stomach, and it made me admire her a bit. Of course, in my self-centered teenage brain, I had to remind myself that the little baby in that tummy was part Ragland and part Markle.

The Markles couldn't take all the credit. I really liked the Ragland family, so it wasn't that much of an issue. Doria got out some cocoa butter, and slowly rubbed it all over her stomach. She said, "It's really great for stretch marks." I was fascinated by the fact that there was a baby in there, and I couldn't wait to see him or her. I wondered why Dad didn't tell me first, but maybe he wanted it to be Doria's surprise. Dad had been unusually quiet for several weeks, and when I thought about it, I realized that the whole thing had a really calming effect on him. The baby would symbolize the beginning of a new family, and our life as an interracial family. I felt like the baby would bring us closer together, instead of feeling like Doria was an outsider. The baby would not be a stepbrother or stepsister because she was the genetic offspring of our dad, like we were. We share the same paternal blood and DNA. I never thought about the baby as a half sibling, and in any family I have ever seen, including friends, I never heard anyone refer to his or her siblings, as half siblings. The baby would be our brother or sister. Similarly, since I only shared half of my DNA with my mother, I never called her my half mother. Baby Meg had a great effect on Dad. He was in such a good mood that he offered to look for a car for me in the newspaper, and also offered to teach me how to drive. Dad purchased an avocado green, 1974 Pinto for me, that had a fuzzy dashboard, and a stick shift that he didn't have the patience to help me learn how to drive. I got in the driver's seat and was nauseous just because I had never driven a stick shift. Dad got in the passenger seat. I thought that opening the door was the biggest mistake of my life, but starting the car was actually the biggest mistake. I was terrible at engaging the clutch. Every time I pushed the clutch in, the car hopped around like a frog, so I guessed that the green color was appropriate. I thought that I was getting PTSD from bouncing around so much, and I was pretty sure my dad was too. I ended up refusing to drive that car, because I had read an article that said, Pintos were exploding when they were rear ended, so I was terrified of driving it. It was a good thing my friend Nicole offered to sell me her little oxidized, automatic, gold Dodge Colt. It wasn't a Jaguar or a Range Rover, but it was mine, and it was a heck of a lot better than taking the bus. Even though I made a little bit of money at the donut shop, my dad paid five hundred dollars for my car. If I was like most teenagers in the Valley whom I had met, I might complain about the fact that my car was cheap, but I couldn't blame my father, or any other parent for not wanting to give a teenager an expensive car, as the first car.

It only made sense to me that expensive cars are to be earned and are for experienced drivers. I was just grateful to have a car, at all. I was elated that I would be learning to drive over the summer. I was imagining all of the places that I could drive my little baby brother or sister to, after I learned how to drive, of course.

Dad and Doria had a gold Peugeot that was attractive, but it made a lot of noise every time it pulled into the driveway. It had a diesel engine that sounded like it had a cluster of tin cans tied to string, bouncing around behind it. To a teenager, noisy engines on parents' cars are good, because they are easy to hear when they come home. Dad was generous anyway, but he was being unusually nice, and I think the baby had a lot to do with it. With a baby on the way, the house was quiet most of the time. On occasion, Doria's friends would breeze in and out through the recreation room. I didn't want to make a big deal out of it, but I didn't understand why there would be strange burning odors, like burning wire, coming from down in the recreation room. Since the house was built in the seventies, I was worried about the wiring in the garage walls, but thankfully, the house never caught fire. I assumed that someone was burning leaves outside.

Time flew quickly, and when the baby was born, we all settled into a routine that was conducive to having a new baby in the house. We all prepared the nest. Even Brandy and Zander, the cats, seemed to know that something was about to change. Doria's stomach got very big, and the swinging bassinet was perfectly dressed with a quilt and side rail padding. Dad must've been nervous because he wasn't getting much sleep. I couldn't help but wonder what she would look like. I wondered if she would look like Dad with thinner lips, or have model perfect lips like Doria, but I knew she would be as cute as a button, no matter who she looked like.

I spoke to Grandma Loveless in the days before the birth, and of course she made derogatory remarks, that were only said in the context of racism. I had already heard those words when I was a kid, and it was enough. It was sad that she could not even be excited about a baby. I could only imagine how many people she probably made feel sad or uncomfortable in her lifetime. As much as I was worried about having to do all the chores in the house, I was relieved to find that Doria had hired a maid. Carlotta did a lot of the mopping and laundry, so that Doria wouldn't have to. Dad helped with chores on the maid's day off. We didn't always have a maid, but it was nice for the time that we did. The Great Migration of 1632 brought our early ancestors to the United

States from England on the Mayflower, and The Ship Lyon, but the great migration of genes brought the Ship Meghan Flower to dock at our house on August 31,1981. My baby sister was bi-racial, beautiful, and was both the color of a peach, and a rose. She had a hypnotizing effect on Dad. *Flower Power* was a hippy slogan in the 1970s, but the term seemed befitting, as a name for the effect that Meghan Flower had on Dad. He seemed to have a half-smile on his face at all times. It was nice to see Dad happy, and at a successful point in his life. Dad often mentioned that he felt like my brother and I didn't have as much as he was able to give Meg, because he wasn't as successful when we were small, but I never thought we went without anything; in fact, I felt as though we were somewhat spoiled. For us as teenagers, it was a relief to have a new baby in the house, and my brother and I thought we could get away with more mischief, because the attention was focused on the baby. Teenagers want more time with their friends, and although we did, it was nice to feel like we had more of a complete family with the baby in the picture.

CHAPTER TWELVE

Inseparable

Dad and Meg were inseparable. Doria lucked out because she had the benefit of more sleep due to the fact that Dad always wore a lot of hats in the family. There was definitely a period where he was both maternal and paternal. From the time she was little, he called her his Bean, which to him, meant a beautiful bean, that would grow into a beautiful baby.

Meg slept in the bassinet next to Dad and Doria's bed until she could roll over. Although we had two cats, Brandy and Xander, it only seemed befitting, that we also got a puppy to complete our big little family. Tom got a puppy and named him Bo Meg was too little, and Bo was too hyper to let him near her at first, but it wasn't long before she was toddling, and playing with him. Doria was a very loving mother. She had such a gentle way with Meg, and so did Dad. Doria would often sing to Meg. I was surprised when I overheard her singing in the bedroom or the hallway. I thought that she had a pretty voice and didn't know it. She had a Brenda Russell album that she would sing to sometimes, and she did such a great job of singing in the bedroom, and to Meg, that I came to like the song. When Meg could sit up and stand, she was moved into her own bedroom, next to Dad and Doria's room. It was the room that was once the office, at the top of the stairs, in the hallway. The wall on the left side of the top of the stairs, was a large built-in cabinet that was home to an amazing collection of records. Since working on *Soundstage* in Chicago, Dad always had great eclectic taste in music. We listened to everything from the music of Judy Collins to Aretha Franklin. Music was almost always playing in our house. Our backyard was not very deep from the patio door to the back wall, but it was wider than the house, and we enjoyed barbecuing outside, or just sitting on the patio, listening to music with Meg.

The weather in Woodland Hills was beautiful in the summer, so our days were spent going for walks with the stroller, playing in the yard, and singing. Digital cameras and cell phones weren't around yet, and we seldom had cameras with us, when we had Kodak moments. I wish I understood, then, the importance of keeping all of those moments in a time capsule. I always wondered what the future would hold for my baby sister. I wondered what the world would be like for her generation.

Like most babies, Meg was speaking more each week, but her words were still baby words that were recognizable by partial syllables. Her facial expressions were funny and seemed punctuated when she spoke. I would often do impersonations of the *Looney Tunes* cartoon character Daffy duck, so her name for me was Dat Duk. How could we not laugh when we were holding her? Her baby laugh was contagious. To add to the list our nicknames, we had Bunky which was Doria's nickname for Dad, Dodi, was Doria's nickname from her youth, Flower, as Doria's nickname for Meg, and on top of my already existing nickname of "Babe," I added, "Daff Duck."

Dad always encouraged us having fun and being creative. He started nurturing Meg's creativity before she was one-year-old by applauding her for throwing blueberries all over the kitchen floor. While most parents would encourage a baby to keep the blueberries on the tray, Dad praised Meg when she threw blueberries around the kitchen. I laughed, and it almost felt therapeutic, throwing food around the kitchen. It was great fun! She laughed, and we all laughed. We didn't laugh about cleaning up the mess though. It was a good thing that the floor all the way through the foyer in the kitchen was blue and white Mediterranean patterned linoleum tile, because it was easy to clean.

When people came to the house, they really couldn't tell it wasn't just a Mediterranean pattern on the floor, but rather a stylish compilation of blueberry stains. Dad gave me some fun ideas for creative play during my babysitting time with Meg. I enjoyed it and I didn't do it for money, of course, because she was my baby sister. One Saturday afternoon, while I was babysitting her, my friend Nicole, came over to the house, which was a nice surprise because she had not visited since Meghan was born. Nicole never mentioned anyone's skin color again because she realized that it was inappropriate, and she was fond of Meg. Meg was toddling, but we still carried her around quite a bit. I had Meg balanced on top of my shoulders, with my arms around her back, so she wouldn't fall.

Nicole was wearing casual clothing and asked me if I wanted to go for a hike to the top of the hill, at the end of our street. Dad and Doria would be home soon, so my babysitting fun would be over. I thought it might be fun to hike, because I was always a bit of a daredevil. Dad and Doria could show up at any moment, so we figured we'd better get all of our girl talk in quickly. Meg was still giggly from being atop my shoulders, because she was higher up than both Nicole and me. I thought she must have loved seeing everything from above, rather than at floor level. Just then, Meg and Nicole looked towards the top of the stairs near Meg's bedroom. I slowly turned, while holding Meg, to see my brother, standing under the hallway light which illuminated his bright copper color hair, undressed, with his private parts tucked in between his legs, making himself appear as a female. His hands were on his hips, and he laughed as he said, "Hello Ladies!". Nicole and I burst into laughter, which made Meg laugh, even though she didn't really know what she was laughing about. Tom hurried around the corner and up the hall to his bedroom. I was embarrassed more for Tom, than I was by Tom, but we had so much fun, that it didn't matter. On the bright side, his behavior was so shockingly feminine in the moment, that considering I had said I wished for a sister back in Santa Monica, when Tom moved in with us, and shared my room, I jokingly said that, I had two sisters. Flower had a fun power over all of us. Even big brother Tom was transformed into a more animated character, when he was around Meg. We knew that Dad and Doria pulled into the driveway because we could hear the diesel engine of the Peugeot.

When the front door opened, Meg reached out for Dad, and Doria. I lifted Meg off of my shoulders, which prompted her little feet to switch in and out of fifth position like a ballerina. I knew her little legs were meant to dance, before she was a year old. Her feet had a very delicate turn out, which made her a great candidate for ballet. Since I had taken ballet classes when I was younger, I was hoping I could teach her a few things when she got a bit older. Nicole was anxious to go hike, but for some reason, I felt a bit reluctant. Dad, Doria, and Meg went upstairs. I didn't want to ruin Nicole's excitement, so I just said, "I hate to do this, but I have a little bit of a stomachache, go ahead and go hiking. I'll just go next time. Can we plan on one-day next week?" She had a disappointed look on her face, so I added, "I promise we will." I didn't want to over commit and under produce, so I knew I was obligated. Nicole went home, and I knew she was bummed out, but I had some things to do in my room, such as folding and putting away clothes, so I went upstairs, to my bedroom and plopped on my bed. The window of my bedroom was open slightly, and there was a nice breeze coming through, causing the cotton lace curtains to sway a little bit. The ambience in the room was so perfect, it was almost ominous.

CHAPTER THIRTEEN

Pandoria's Box

As I lay in my bed watching the curtains dance with the breeze, I gazed at the music boxes on top of my dresser. I had several music boxes that had little ballerinas inside of them, dancing under glass domes. I felt such a sense of peace and serenity in my room.

My music box trance was interrupted by the chirping of a little voice approaching my bedroom, and Doria's voice carrying from their bedroom down the hall. "Babe, Flower is coming down the hallway!" she yodeled. As I was getting up, I could see Meg's little eyes, and dark curly eyelashes, on her hands and knees, peeking around the door into my room. It always made me laugh when her eyebrows went up, and she grinned. Her little expressions are the endearing subjects of some of my fondest memories.

I walked over and picked her up, straddling her on my hip with my arm around her as we walked over to the dresser, got one of the music boxes down, and carried it over to the bed. With Meg seated on my lap, I reached in front of her, and turned the music box on. She loved watching the little ballerina spin around, as the stem inside jutted upwards repeatedly. As I looked at her, there was so much I wanted to say, but she was so little, I knew that if I rambled on, in her own baby way, she might enjoy it, but she wouldn't understand what I was talking about. I thought it was best just to listen to the music box.

As the ballerina and her partner danced, they seemed to take on a life of their own inside the dome. I knew then, that someday I would give Meg a couple of my music boxes when she was older. Zander the fat cat loved to come lie on my bed. He was such a gentle cat. He didn't get nervous or jittery around Meg.

Doria came into my bedroom carrying a magazine, opened it towards the back, and showed me a small print advertisement for a mood ring. Mood rings were a novelty jewelry items that were a big hit in the 1970's, they would change colors on the finger, as the body temperature changed.

I got up with Meg, put the music box back on the dresser and let it play until it wound down. "What's that?" I asked. "I'm selling jewelry! I started the new company!" she proudly exclaimed. "Wow what's the company name?" I asked. "Three Cherubs," she said, in a high pitched, pompous tone. I stood back and thought about it for a second. "That's a cool name," I replied curiously. The entire moment felt very uncomfortable. I handed Meg to Doria and sat back down. When I asked her what "Three Cherubs" represented, my curiosity was quickly extinguished. In an unexpected dismissal, she uttered, "It stands for, Me, Flower, and Bunky." In an awkward moment of silence, I couldn't help but realize, that her concept excluded my brother and me.

I felt hurt by that but didn't want to let it show. As much as we were wanting a unified family, it was obvious at that moment, that she wanted to move us over, and have a family that excluded my brother and me. The idea seemed so inappropriate, because she'd moved into our lives, we did not move into hers. Although I wanted to be positive about having a sense of family unity, I knew that there was another agenda lurking in the shadows. As weeks went by, Doria built her business up to being able to afford her renting a kiosk in the Topanga Plaza Mall. It seemed like it was turning out to be more expensive than it was worth, compared to the profits and the time spent being there. She also traveled to art festivals, and clothing shows, taking some of her sundresses, and her accessories around.

I was hoping that it would be a growing business for her, but even though I was hoping she would recruit my brother and I to help a little bit, she just wanted to do her own thing. I didn't usually pay much attention to Doria coming in and out of the house with her friends, because I had become familiar with a few of them. Sometimes they would buzz through the door, laughing and chattering.

On that particular day, I sat in my bedroom, with so much steam coming out of my ears, that nothing in my closet would be wrinkled. I was upset thinking about the partying that went on when my dad was not home. I tiptoed downstairs to investigate the commotion. When I got to the foyer, I saw a couple of people coming upstairs out of the recreation room, and into the foyer area. I made my way downstairs to say hello. Doria's friends were having a jolly time and all were smiling. Every time Doria made a trip to Humboldt County, the days following seemed to be filled with what looked like group therapy in the recreation room. I only became uncomfortable with it because I didn't know how to tell my father what was going on, without him thinking I was being dramatic. I resented feeling like I had to keep a secret at home.

When Dad and Doria were not home, and Meg was asleep in her crib, I hurried nervously into their bedroom, because I still thought they could be home at any time. I opened the dresser drawers quietly, to look for any morsel of evidence that might explain the climate change in the household. I came across something in the back corner of one of the drawers, that shocked me into nausea. I picked up a small stack of photographs, and I couldn't believe my eyes! The picture on the railroad tracks, hanging in the hallway was tolerable, because I could justify it as being tasteful. I looked through the pictures quickly, and a lot of the behaviors in the house started making sense, including the squabbling. I wondered about some of the women in the photographs with Doria, and grimaced over the implications. I hurriedly tried to put the photographs back as neatly as I had found them and closed the drawer. I felt like an archaeologist who had just uncovered Pandoria's Box and left it in place.

The antique dresser drawer had been the keeper of hidden secrets, and after my little archaeological dig, so would I. I walked around with the constant smirk on my face, but I felt guilty about peeking in the drawer. I don't know why I felt guilty about peeking in drawers though. On several occasions I noticed that things in my bedroom drawers had been misplaced.

I didn't know who the villain was, but I was determined to let them know that I was aware of their snooping. I got out several sheets of paper and on the first piece of paper I wrote, "What you're looking for is in drawer number two." I put that piece of paper in the top drawer. For each drawer I put a note in it indicating that what was being searched for was in the following drawer.

I thought, at minimum, if someone was going to be snooping through my drawers that it should feel like a game, at least for me. I never did figure out who it was, but I got a laugh out of it in any case.

CHAPTER FOURTEEN

Darkness and Silence

I was becoming more and more of an adventuresome teenager, staying out sometimes after my 10:30 curfew, and I was certainly a daredevil. I knew I couldn't get out of hiking with Nicole, and I promised her I would go after declining earlier. It was just my luck that a beautiful sunny Saturday rolled around, and Nicole was at my door in a T-shirt and khaki cargo pants, ready to hike up the hill.

I was always one to challenge gravity. I never felt I could run fast enough or jump high enough. I suppose I was at an age that contributed to feeling that I was impervious to the elements. Nicole was as adventuresome as I was and had a seemingly immortal energy. I was happy to see her at my door, and she didn't have to coerce me into going.

I thought I could use some rigorous exercise, so we walked up the street, to the end of the cul-de-sac. With an anxious glance, she pointed to the top of the steep hill which was only accessible by climbing upwards through a lot of bushes and large rocks. I thought I was Wonder Woman, and there was nothing I couldn't handle, so I chuckled and said "Let's go!" Even though I thought I was athletic, I was doubting myself halfway up the hill, and I started seeing stars. Because it was extremely hot outside, and the sun was very bright, I was concerned about how long I would last before I withered. I didn't want to make a fool out of myself. After all, I had to blend in. When we got to the top of the hill, I was out of breath, and squinting to avoid the direct sun beaming into my eyes. I was surprised to see a group of sweaty teenage boys, who looked like they just walked off the set of Dukes of

Hazzard as extras, laughing and horsing around by their Hot-Rods. They were very rough around the edges. Several of them looked over at Nicole and me and laughed as they pointed at us. I could tell by the doubting smirks on their faces, that they thought because we were girls, we were not tough enough to get on the swing. I was feeling the need to change that misperception. The giant tree was perfect for a Robinson Crusoe style treehouse. Its grandly poised branches seemed to hang out over the cliff as a dance invitation to the entire neighborhood. Hanging from one of the limbs was a long firehose, that was used by kids in the area as a swing. The goal was to grab a hold of it and swing out over the cliff like *Tarzan*, and then swing back. Although I had never danced with a tree, or a firehose, I thought it would be funny to watch.

Nicole looked at me suggestively, and asked "Are you sure you want to do this?" I thought it would be easy enough, so I said, "I'm in like Flynn"! I was reluctant but wouldn't admit it. With an exaggerated feeling of false bravado, I grabbed ahold of the firehose, walked back as far as I could, and got a running start, before I jumped off the cliff, and swung out as far as I could. I laughed as I felt myself gliding weightlessly off of the hill, and skyward above the street. I enjoyed it so much that it gave me an endorphin high. It was so exhilarating that I looked forward to doing it again, after others had taken their turns.

The second time out was great, and I had what seemed like an illegal amount of fun. Like the old saying, "The third time's a charm." I looked at some of the people standing around, then at Nicole, and said, "Watch me, knowing me, I'm going to fall this time!" Everything around me seemed to move in slow motion for a moment. Nicole laughed because she knew I was pretty strong enough to make it the third time out. I grabbed the hose, took a running start, hoisted myself up, wrapped my legs around it, and felt weightless, as I was propelled over the edge and slightly upwards, seeing only the blue sky above me. All I remembered after that, was my hand slipping. I felt nothing as I hit the ground, and then, as if my life had stopped, I saw nothing but darkness, and I heard only silence. I felt like I was in a flotation chamber. I set out to change a stereotype but changed my whole life instead. An hour later, I woke up on the ground, at the bottom of the hill. The sweaty, befuddled faces of several teenage boy critters I had never seen before, were staring wide-eyed at me as they hovered over me. I couldn't believe that I fell the third time out. Even when I felt fatigued, I thought I could sustain the suspension, but my arms just let go, and I had no awareness of hitting the ground. When I awoke, I looked at Nicole and asked her what happened. Her sensitive calm, even in the crisis, reminded me of Grandma Markle. She was very focused and soft-spoken. She knelt down beside me and used her t-shirt to dab some blood off my forehead. I didn't have a whole lot of feeling in my back, but I could feel some sticks and rocks working their way into my skin. It became less comfortable as I woke up a bit. "We have to get you out of here and get you to my house," she said. I was trying to figure out how to tell my dad what had happened, but instead, I decided to go Nicole's house with her, until I could feel better and figure out what to do. It seemed as though out of nowhere, one of the teenage boys pulled up beside us in his hot rod car, and he and Nicole helped me get up, brush debris off of me, and get into the front passenger seat. The rest of the kids scattered into the distance. I was still a bit dizzy. I took a deep breath and put my head back until we got to Nicole's house. The house was a three story, very expensive home built on a hillside in the 1970s, and it was nothing short of a Frank Lloyd Wright design. Her father was a musician in the 1960's, so he made a very good living. Nicole helped me walk slowly to the top of the stairs, and then she opened the door. We were relieved that her father and stepmother were not home. I wouldn't want them to worry that they were responsible for me, and I wouldn't want to have to explain what we just did.

Nicole helped me to lie down on the bed in her parents' bedroom that was completely ensconced in mirrors, and then she walked out for a few minutes. I looked up and my throbbing headache was worsened by trying to figure out the reasoning behind mirrors on the ceiling too.

When Nicole returned, she had a bottle of Vodka in one hand,

and some Band-Aids in the other. Although she wasn't even a nursing student, I was really impressed with her attention to detail, especially the need for using antiseptic, and for also binding the skin back together, with a butterfly Band-Aid, as securely as if it had been stitched, so that it would heal. It was about a 3inch gash just above the left side of my temple in my hairline.

I had to call home, but was worried about being grounded, which was probably unnecessary, because Dad would be worried about me and not mad. I should have gone directly to the hospital, but instead I chose to avoid it. Nicole handed me her phone, and I called home. Dad was at work, so I told Doria what happened, and that I would be spending the night at Nicole's house. According to my father, Doria called him at work and gave him the information.

Over the next couple of days, I lost vision in my left eye, and every time I took a step with my left foot, it felt as though I was stepping into a hole. I was rapidly losing more of my balance, and coordination on the left side of my body. I knew it was time to see a doctor, when I almost collapsed, while climbing the hallway stairs.

My father took me to a nearby hospital, and I had an MRI. MRI technology was not very good yet, and the neurologist wasn't sure what was causal in my impaired mobility. At first we thought I had a concussion, but further diagnostic testing suggested the possibility of MS, and I was put on high doses of prednisone, to halt what I was told was an MS attack, which was theoretically triggered by my fall.

It was overwhelmingly scary. I had frequently ignored tingling sensations and numbness in my legs as growing stress. No one in the family tree had ever been disabled that I was aware of, so I thought, surely I could not have a disabling condition.

CHAPTER FIFTEEN

What Doesn't Kill You Makes You Stronger

I was a typical teenage girl, worried about my weight, instead of being worried about my health. I was freaked out, because the prednisone forced me to retain water, and I gained ten sizes over a two-month period. I was just starting to lose my teenage baby fat, and get in shape, and then before I knew it, I was so bloated that, when I looked in the mirror, it appeared as though my head was pulled down slightly over a stump, because my neck was so wide.

My hands looked like blown up rubber gloves. I just looked in the mirror and cried, because I didn't know how long the effects of the steroids would last. I was lucky that my fall didn't kill me but, at times, I wished it had. It was really difficult as a teenager to observe how people looked at me, or avoided looking at me. I sometimes heard people whispering rude remarks about my weight as I walked past them.

There was a young man I'd met who wanted to date me, but when he showed up at the door to visit, and he saw me that size, he gasped as he shrieked, "Great seeing' ya!" With that, he turned around, hurried away, and vanished into the sunset. I never saw him again.

Instead of being worried about me, or what happened, he was offended that I was overweight. I never believed that stereotypes about weight were so influential, until then. Being heavier taught me a lot about people. It also taught me that I should stop worrying so much about my looks and worry about my health. I also learned to avoid making assumptions about people who appear heavy. Regardless of the reason for being heavy, people don't deserve to be harshly judged because of body weight.

It's only fair to consider that some people like being heavier, and people should be free and comfortable to live and look as they wish. Beauty really is in the eye of the beholder. There was a time when society equated being heavier with being beautiful. During the 1600's in Rubenesque era, named after artist Peter Paul Rubens, who painted plump, voluptuous bodies as the cool trendy thing. Beauty is in the eye of the beholder was a cliché that I always believed in, and I tried to look at body shapes and sizes through the eyes of others.

What I was going through reminded me of the Janis Ian song, *Seventeen*. I knew the teenage years were difficult, but between 16 and 18 are probably the toughest, because we try and fit into adult beauty standards that are often unrealistic, and that we can seldom measure up to. That year was difficult and eye-opening for me, for several reasons. I felt that the world is often unkind to people who are not physically attractive by social norms.

I felt like I was stereotyped as a fat person, and it changed not only the way I saw people who don't live up to beauty standards, but it changed my attitudes about beauty standards in general. At the same time, I was also dealing with the social stereotypes of disability lurking. Even though I had a fall that likely triggered the onset of MS, I was still in such denial that I could be disabled at any point in my life, because I was always so active. I knew that there were lessons in everything I was going through, and I thought it was important, that I be a trooper, because I was no more special than so many people who live with physical limitations, especially those who are children. That being said, I thought it would be an insult for me to feel like I didn't deserve the hardships that I was having. I didn't think anybody deserves injury or disability, but I knew that I was certainly not entitled to be exempt from disability. Having a human body means being fragile, and most people will deal with some sort of physical challenge in their lifetime.

I didn't want to focus on physical appearance, but I was once terrified of disability, because at many times through my life, I had seen people make fun of people in wheelchairs, and I had heard stories of caregiver and institutional abuse, and neglect of people with disabilities. I felt that people, in general, are not very empathetic when it comes to physical difference, especially disability.

After witnessing rude or intolerant social responses to disability, I always thought it would be great if high schools, and junior high schools, allowed students to role-play for a week in wheelchairs, not only to educate students, but perhaps to foster empathy and minimize stereotypes before adulthood. A program like that would also allow students and faculty to experience how difficult limited accessibility is, and maybe they could make appropriate modifications and improvements in their schools. It is especially important during the teenage years to be able to empathize with others, and maybe walk in his or her shoes, or roll in his or her wheelchair for a week. It would give able bodied students the ability to experience how difficult physical limitations are, and it could help young people to see how socially marginalizing or, conversely, empowering disability can be, if it is managed properly. I had a feeling that I would be in a wheelchair someday. After my fall, I realized that life can change in a split second. I was too afraid to go back to school until I lost my steroid bloat, so I pulled out of school to recover. I knew that I could resume my education at any point. I also had to think about making money, as I got closer to age 18.

Disability was scary to think about, largely because I didn't want to be a burden to my family. Doria was in her own world and she was busy with the baby, so I didn't ask her for help. She knew what I was dealing with. I was hoping for a little moral support, but instead it felt more like a disconnect.

Nicole was coming by frequently to help me, and to make sure that I was OK. She had become my best friend. We swore that after we died, we would meet back at the top of the hill and laugh about it all. I hoped I would never have to see that day, too early. Aside from Nicole coming by and keeping my spirits up, I had another good friend whom I had met in the neighborhood, who was extremely handsome, but we were both awkwardly inexperienced in romantic relationships, and so we were perfectly suited to being just friends.

Brad came over the house on a regular basis, just to cheer me up, and he became like a family member to the extent that even Doria and Dad were used to seeing him at the house. It was great to have a close male friend who didn't care how I looked, because he liked me for who I was. We could be open with each other about anything.

He made the comment in an awkward tone of voice one day that Doria was looking at him. I laughed because, although he was incredibly handsome, he was a teenager, and she was married to my dad. Doria could be quite funny and very animated. I couldn't understand what he meant, until I saw it in action one day. I thought she was joking. Brad was so handsome that everywhere we went, women would stop and stare at him, but he was very shy, and not mature yet in terms of his interaction with women. He looked like Jan Michael Vincent. He was the sweetest guy, but we were not attracted to each other at all, so it was kind of funny watching women ogle him. I really enjoyed having a great-looking male friend, whom I knew would not flirt with me either. I felt a nice sense of safety with that.

I came through the front door with him after going to the beach one day and we passed Doria as she was coming down the stairs. I wondered if she had smoked pot, because she looked at him with a drawn out glance, as she smiled and said, "Hi Brad," in a playful tone of voice. He turned bright red, and we hurried down into the recreation room. Brad wouldn't stop whispering about how embarrassed he was. I never told my father about it, but it seemed like overt flirting, and Brad didn't want to come by the house for several weeks.

My first and only personal experience with pot happened one afternoon, when I found my brother and a couple of his friends sitting on the sofa with a bong on the table in front of them. I knew what it was, but I was in shock that they would just have it out in the open. My brother decided to take the opportunity to make a spectacle of me in front of his friends, and so he said, "I bet you don't know what this is."

I said, "Yes I do, it's a bong." Then he took it one step further, and said, "Bet you can't handle it." I was so irritated by his arrogance, that I decided to give him a run for his money. I looked at his friends, and then at him, and I said, "I'll tell you what boys, I'm going to smoke all of you under the table." So my brother put the match to the bong, and I inhaled it. I thought I was cool, so I did it about 10 times. I could feel my skin become cold and clammy, and beading with perspiration, as I looked at my brother. "Okay amateurs, I can't soar with eagles, if I hang out with turkeys, so I'm outta her," I gasped. With the ease of a sandbag, I soared upstairs, trying not to faint or throw up. I felt my veins trying to push out through my skin, and I could barely breathe. I had always seen people laugh and smile when they smoked, but laughing or smiling was nowhere in my dictionary, or in my plans at that moment.

I slept for a couple of hours, and then when I woke up, I vowed never to smoke pot again. It was a morbid experience for me. That was a great part of my teenage years for a lot of reasons. I learned so much about my strengths, and my weaknesses. I learned that what doesn't kill you makes you stronger, and that I was a master at keeping secrets.

I became very sensitive to the smell of smoke after that and swore that I was allergic to it. My shock therapy experience was good, in that I never wanted to try it again.

Shadows Dancing on the Walls

Everything in the household was going smoothly, with Doria running her little Three Cherubs costume jewelry and sundress business out of the home, and also working a part time job as a telephone reservationist for the travel industry. My brother Tom was working at Lulu's flower store, just around the corner from our house, and Dad, of course, worked at ABC TV. I recovered from my physical disability, at least for the time being. I started jogging a couple of miles every day, and I assumed that the doctor was a quack, and that what I was told about MS, was a misdiagnosis, because I was so athletic.

Dad and Doria seemed to get along cordially, until Meg started preschool. Dad enrolled her at The Little Red School House, which would be a great place to fast track her into private education, amongst great faculty and kids, many of whom were celebrities' kids in Los Angeles. It was near ABC TV in Hollywood, so Dad could drop Meg off, and then go to work, and pick her up at the end of the day.

I explored extra work which meant that I was a non-distinct part of the crowd around a main character, and bit parts with a few speaking lines as an actress on *General Hospital*, and a new television show called *A Different World*.

Dad's friend, Kay was intelligent, and beautiful. I was so impressed with her style, but more than that, I was really impressed with her kindness, and friendship. She was incredibly mature and easy to talk to. She was becoming a good friend of ours, and I came to learn that she really cared about my dad, in a much deeper way, than as only a friend. It was through Kay that I became more aware of the fact that my Dad and Doria were not getting along, and she confided in me how it was that my father and Doria got together. After spending time at her home, hanging out with her son one afternoon, she drove me home, and when we pulled up to the driveway, she let me know how much Doria had manipulated my father when they first met. "Babe, Doria had your Dad jumping through hoops, getting him French fries or whatever she wanted at lunchtime" she teased. I couldn't imagine that Doria's wraparound skirt and smile would be so persuasive, but for whatever reason, Dad obliged her, and went across the street to get her lunch, not realizing that he was making a complete fool out of himself in front of all the women, witnessing the rat chase the carrot on the stick.

My suggestion would have been that she find a new hobby, but my father was apparently charmed into a compliant stupor. I was horrified to find out that she was using him to fetch lunch. I was starting to see what I thought was a motive, and I didn't like it. Only dogs fetch, I thought.

I really wished that my father would have chosen Kay to marry, but it didn't work out that way. I had a sick feeling in my stomach, and suddenly all of the partying and shopping excursions started to make sense. I was dying to tell Kay about what I found in the drawer, but there never seemed to be the right time. If I didn't want to find myself in deep doo-doo, I had to be quiet. Although Dad seldom swore, I began hearing expletives exchanged in the hallway, as Doria was passing, and I could sense that my Dad was sad. As I heard those things, the secrets that were hiding in the drawer, seemed to be standing atop my shoulders, whispering to me to free them from captivity. I tried not to be too nosy, but I should've known that the partying with friends, and going up North to Humboldt County might have been causal in the beginning of a breakdown in the marriage. I could really feel for my Dad, because I knew that it must've bothered him when she was visiting friends up North, and at least he had the comfort of Kay, and a good friendship to lean on during those times.

Teenagers are not usually privy to that stuff, but they understand what's going on, even in passing. I really thought that my dad was being used, and I couldn't see the marriage lasting very long. I thought it would be hard on my sister, but Doria and Dad had a plan for trying to make it so that she knew she was loved by both of them, even if they couldn't get along. I wasn't really stumbling on things that would point me in an interesting direction, but I knew I needed to think seriously about my own future. I was very outspoken so Dad suggested I try a course in broadcasting. We found a small broadcasting school that was near ABC T.V. The location was perfect, because I could often have lunch with my father at our favorite Japanese restaurant near the studio, after class.

It was there that I learned broadcasting in the school of hard knocks way, when pronunciation has to be precise, broadcasters have to wear many hats, and FCC regulations were stricter about what could be said on the air. I was optimistic, that if I didn't return to school for a while, I knew I found something that I would be good at, and that didn't necessarily require physical agility, if I had challenges with disability. I completed the broadcasting program with flying colors.

Radio jobs were scarce at that time and I needed a regular job. Like most young people in Los Angeles, I took the quickest job I could get that was flexible, and that was waiting tables. It wasn't glamorous work, but I actually enjoyed it, because I was getting paid to run around all day, flirt, and have fun. After my brush with death, I wanted to be on my feet all day. I felt like Forrest Gump, in that I was running all the time, just because I could, and it was quite a task just to get me to sit down for any length of time.

I felt like I had to seize every moment, and squeeze in as much as I could. I wanted to make sure that I was choosing the best career for me, because I knew that for any of us, life can be shortened at any given moment.

When teenagers are becoming adults, it's common at least in the United States, for them to get their own apartments. My brother found a little place on Topanga Canyon Boulevard that he rented, but I wanted to be close to West Hollywood and the beach, so I found a great little apartment straight out of the 1920's in Westwood, adjacent to the UCLA campus and trendy

Westwood stores.

Even though my brother and I had our apartments, I was always within 10 minutes of the house, and I could go with Dad to pick Meghan up at The Little Red School House. I had a fun part time job as a waitress at a French restaurant, and another at a trendy clothing store. At times I felt like it was grasping for straws, and I had to do as much as I could before I became disabled. I wondered how many other people with a disability, or the perception of limited time, felt the same way as I did. I didn't know anyone who had experienced a disability or a serious injury, so I felt very alone. I was afraid to talk to anyone about it, because I thought it would make me look less than fabulous. A lot of people didn't want to hear about other people's challenges or problems, so I typically kept things quiet and tried to be as positive as I could around others.

CHAPTER SEVENTEEN

Westwood

My apartment in Westwood was a very small studio apartment, with one large room, a tiny bathroom, and a very small kitchen, with a window that looked out over the swimming pool of a fraternity house. It should've been fun for any young woman to look out into the backyard of a fraternity house, but it always seemed that when I had the least amount of sleep, I could hear the fraternity brothers, screaming and jumping off of the roof, and into the swimming pool, after consuming massive quantities of alcohol. I learned to keep my window blinds closed because they didn't always land in the swimming pool. The main room of my apartment had a large bay window and a patio that led to it. I could always hear Meg laugh, when she and Dad walked up the stairs to knock on my door.

The wall outside my apartment building had a lot of bright pink flowers, growing up the wall on creeping vines. Meg loved to pick them whenever she came over to visit. Although Dad and Doria dressed her, Meg seemed to enjoy stylish clothing, and put on her own accessories. Even at such a small age, her clothing was always perfectly clean and pressed. Dad made sure that her wardrobe came from the best stores. Meg knew who the designer Betsey Johnson was before I did.

To say that Meg simply liked to pick flowers would be an understatement. When she came to my apartment, there was a long stairway leading up to my balcony that had bright pink flowers that resembled giant Morning Glories on the vines that covered the stairway wall. She would gaze at them dreamily and want to pick them all.

During that time, I thought that Flower was a perfect nickname for her, especially when I saw her light up and giggle as she held them. Meg was so pretty as she blossomed. Some moments in time we'll never get back, but it's great that they are immortalized in photography. It was always Dad to the rescue with the camera.

Dad and Doria had made the transition to living in two separate apartments. Doria lived in Los Angeles, on the second floor of the duplex, and Dad took a place in Hollywood hills, not too far from Capitol Records. He also had a little apartment on Prospect Avenue across from ABC, but he only used it as a crash pad, when his schedule on *General Hospital* was so tedious that he needed to squeeze in two or three hours of sleep before starting again.

I was really excited to hear that Meg started taking acting classes in North Hollywood. I would often go with Dad to pick her up from class, when I was not working, and I could tell then that she loved the art of pretend. The teacher regularly bragged to Dad that Meg was talented and well liked. As I was sitting in the backseat of Dad's car waiting for her to get out of class, she climbed into the front seat, in what seemed like a state of euphoria. I teased her about the idea of boys in her class liking her, and she blushed. "Hey Meg, I bet all the boys like you, don't they? "Only a couple of them," she replied. I loved seeing her self-awareness develop, but more than that, she seemed to have a cynical sense of humor about it.

Between The Little Red School House, and her acting classes, she was becoming quite a character. I think school was a great buffer from the fact that Dad and Doria were divorcing. Meg seemed happy, and oblivious to any inconvenience associated with living in between two households. Dad tried to make things fun and always explained it as having two houses with one bridge. Although divorce could've been really difficult, it seemed as though it was handled in such a way as to not only reinforce that she was loved by everybody, but she had such healthy distractions and environmental stimuli, that it seemed to strengthen her. The Little Red School House was where Meg met her first best friend, who was somewhat of her classroom twin.

Dad always raved that her parents were lovely and seemed to also enjoy the fact that the girls were like Siamese twins. When I would say, "Meg you and Nikki look so much alike, she could sleep in your bed, and Dad would think she was you. You could sleep in her bed at her house, and her parents would think you were her!" she laughed, but once she said surprisingly, "She can't be me." It seemed really grandiose that that would be her response. But kids say the darnedest things. I was almost certain that they would be lifelong best friends. She had no idea then that a best friend is the one person who would know the most intimate details about her. Nikki was never the gossipy type though. I wondered if Meg and Nikki would get old together, and look-alike, even as older women. There's no better friendship than that of a friend you grow old with. I was really hoping that I would maintain contact with my friend Nicole until we were older. My real best friends were my father and my grandmother. I could always rely on them for advice that wasn't tied into peer pressure and, even though family members can be critical to some degree, I felt that their advice was sound, because they loved me. Of course there was some things specific to being a woman that I wouldn't speak to my brother about but, for the most part, he was always there and supportive. If I was emotionally stoic at times, it was only because I didn't want to disappoint my father.

CHAPTER EIGHTEEN

Baby Momma

I was always a fan of outdoor adventure and felt as though I could never run far enough, or jump high enough, or stay in the water long enough. I didn't just want a career but I was really feeling the need to do something outdoors that I had never done.

I wanted to be near snow. After dealing with disability, I was feeling the need to defy gravity and push myself physically with a new sporting adventure. I wanted to ski.

I called my buddy Nicole to discuss the idea with her. I was hoping that she would want to go because she loved skiing. I was really worried because I couldn't get a hold of her. I knew she would've been excited for me. I left a message with her stepmother several times.

One brisk November day, I walked out onto my balcony, and sat on the ledge, fidgeting with a piece of ivy pensively in between my fingers. West Los Angeles was beautiful, but I was wanting something more. I could not afford to go to Switzerland, but I loved the snow, and so on that happy note, a friend and I decided to go to Lake Tahoe. I gave notice at my job, had my rent paid up for the month, because I was just renting month-to-month, so on a whim, my friend and I had her brother drive us to Lake Tahoe, knowing that we would have to get there and start looking for jobs.

My friend's brother, who was smitten with me, drove us there and ended up staying for a week. Suffice it to say, the sunlight dancing on the snow early in the day, the moonlight waltzing across the snow at night, and a bottle of champagne were intoxicating, and we ended up playing Twister while George Winston music played. Not only did we wake up wondering how and when we got undressed below the sleeping bag, but we were as physically intertwined, as if a tornado had put us into those positions. After realizing that we both felt ridiculously embarrassed over what happened, he went back to Southern California, and I had to get serious about finding a temporary job.

I only planned to be there through the season, but I wasn't independently wealthy, so I had to work. I searched the help wanted ads and I panicked, because I didn't want to work at a casino, and there wasn't a lot I could do in the snow. I wasn't an avid skier yet, so I couldn't work at the ski slopes, and I didn't foresee having any time to ski in the near future. I almost gave up my search, when I came across an ad that said a local radio station needed a morning news caster.

Since my father had put me through broadcasting school, and I figured that I had nothing to lose, I bundled up, and took a nice long hike in the snow to the little radio station, to see if I could get some kind of job there. I loved what I had learned in broadcasting school, I knew that I could apply those skills somewhere. When I got there, it was freezing cold outside, but delightfully warm inside, and furthermore, I was pleased to find that, unlike his intimidating baritone radio voice, the news director was small in stature, nerdy, and I started to feel like I might have a chance at getting the job. He stared curiously at me and asked whether or not I had any demo tapes. I panicked, because I had never actually been on the air, other than in the classroom. I was good at panicking, and even better at covering the fact that I was panicking. Enthusiastically, I looked at him and said "I don't, but why don't you just put me on the air, and let me show you what I can do?" I adhered to the old saying, "Never let them see you sweat," so I just grinned. He looked at me like I was crazy. Then he stood up, pointed to the music wall, and said, "Go for it." With that in mind, I nervously looked around the booth for songs on cartridge at the time, pulled a couple of commercial spots, and set them on the table. I went to the AP News machine, and tore a couple of pages off it, then circled one or two stories.

After creating what I thought was a decent half hour, I took my headphones off, smiled nervously. After a long pregnant pause, he said, "Well thank you for coming" and "We will be in touch." I felt like a puppy dog, leaving the radio station with my tail between my legs. I was thinking the worst, the whole way back to my cabin.

The snow was falling heavily and I knew there was a blizzard coming in. After having a cup of hot cocoa and daydreaming as I watched the snowfall for hours, I climbed in my sleeping bag and fell asleep. The following morning, I was still in my thermal Long Johns, having my coffee and stressing about finding a job. I nearly spilled coffee all over myself when I heard violent pounding on my front door.

I didn't have any neighbors very close by, so the only person I could think was at my door during a blizzard would be some wandering maniac. I carefully tiptoed to the door, and pretended to have a man's voice, so whoever was behind the door wouldn't think that I was a female alone in the house. In a deep baritone voice I asked, "Who is it?!" I was extremely nervous. I couldn't hear anything on the other side of the door, because the wind was howling loudly. As I leveraged all of my weight against the door, and opened it slightly, I saw a man with a scarf over his face, gasping as he was trying to say something. I thought he might be hurt or needing help of some kind. I could hardly understand him, but I figured it out. "You got the job! Start tomorrow!" he uttered. I was so excited, that I slammed the door. It took me a few minutes to realize that in my excitement, I had just slammed the door on my new boss.

I hurriedly opened the door, apologized, and thanked him. He waved as he hurried to his car. I closed the door and jumped up and down excitedly. What started out feeling like a Stephen King film, ended up feeling like a Stephen Sondheim musical.

I danced and sang around my little living room until I was exhausted. I couldn't wait to tell everybody that I got hired to work in radio. It was a good thing he hired me, because I had no money, I was literally down to eating pasta with canned corn with no seasoning. I was proud of myself for taking the chance. I was insecure on and off throughout my life, especially because of disability, but I learned from that experience, that during times when I didn't believe in myself, it was important to keep moving forward. I got to the point where I was really enjoying the radio station, and had worked out a system, such that the news was flowing smoothly. I set my alarm as usual for two in the morning, so I could get up and walk two miles to the radio station. As difficult as it seemed, it was a tremendous amount of fun, getting up while it was still pitch black outside and walking such a distance in the snow. I would usually jump up in the morning because I couldn't wait to get on the air, but when I sat up, I felt both dizzy and nauseous. The whole scenario was telegraphing and I knew that this day would be pivotal in my life somehow. I thought, "Uh oh, I must be getting my period." Then it dawned on me that I was two weeks late.

Like Grandma Markle, I was able to look at just about anything as an adventure and a blessing. I could really have fun amidst great challenge, and for me, it was the challenges that made life fun.

After I had a cup of coffee, I remembered the 1970's game, Twister. It didn't require a scientific calculator to do the math. Waking up with a man in my sleeping bag, an empty bottle of champagne on the windowsill, bodies intertwined, and my clothing lying on the floor clear across the room, suggested the possibility that pregnancy was imminent. I knew I had to go into work, and then go to the grocery store or pharmacy and get a pregnancy test after my shift. I didn't know what I was going to say my father because going to Lake Tahoe was already shocking to him.

Later in the day, I got the test and it was positive. I thought I had a good job, and although I didn't have a car yet, I was sure I could make it work and have a baby. I was trying to be optimistic, and whether I stayed in Lake Tahoe or not, I knew I had to tell Chris. It wasn't like it was only my decision, and since he was the father, it was only the right thing to do. I knew I had to get back to Los Angeles.

When I called Chris, he was very dismissive and said he had to work. When I told him what happened, and that I was having a baby, he wanted nothing to do with the baby, or me. I didn't expect an instant relationship, but I expected some empathy, and an acknowledgement of shared responsibility. I wanted a woman's advice, rather than my father's. I tried calling Nicole, but there was no answer.

Grandma Markle was in Florida with a companion, so I was afraid to burden her. I called Grandma Loveless. I was hoping to hear her say that she loved me and would help with whatever I needed. Because I knew what happened to her; being left with a child during the war, I certainly thought she would be understanding. I told her that I was having a baby, and the words out of her mouth were colder and more vile than what she uttered when I was in first grade. "Abort the thing," was her heinous suggestion.

I stood there, sad and numb, but I wasn't numb because my feet were frozen in the snow, I was numb because I was heartbroken and horrified that my own grandmother would rather me abort my own child, than have the child. I loved kids, and because she had been so nice to me throughout my childhood, I thought she did too. I remembered that she was cold and heartless when Meg was being born.

I couldn't believe she would make rude racial remarks about a baby, so I shouldn't have been shocked by her telling me to have an abortion. I reminded myself that she was probably trying to be protective in her own distorted way. She probably thought that since I was a single mom, that the baby would be better off not being born.

Whatever was going through her head, I thought it was cruel and disgusting. She said, "I'm going to send you the money for an abortion." Although I had no intention of having an abortion, I agreed to let her send me the money, which I would use somehow for the baby.

So many young women around the world have experienced what I was going through and it is a frightening position to be in. I was afraid and, yet, I love children and couldn't imagine terminating the life of a beautiful baby. I couldn't tell my father just now, and decided to wait until I had a solid plan, or until the baby was born. Although I didn't have her with me, I could remember Grandma Markle saying "Just take things day by day and make the best of it." That was very basic old-fashioned advice that got a lot of people through the depression. In reality, we have no choice other than making the best that we can out of life circumstances. I also like the old saying "When life hands you lemons, make lemonade." I had visions of myself sitting at a lemonade stand, selling cups of frozen lemonade in the snow.

As my stomach grew bigger and I was visibly pregnant, people were just too busy to stop and offer help of any kind. I was always the kind of person who would help someone in need, even if it was to help them pick up groceries that they had dropped.

I realized that the world had changed in that. Emile Durkheim would say that people were driven by rugged individualism, unlike the days when people would knock on your door and bring chicken soup if they knew you were sick. Neighbors used to care about one another.

I felt like the elderly people that I had encountered over my lifetime, who pointed out the rhetorical fact that times have changed, and I wondered how much worse the world would get in terms of rugged individualism, racism, and stereotypes in my lifetime.

CHAPTER NINETEEN

Angels Around Me

I was afraid to go back to Los Angeles because it is expensive, and I had no friends who could help me by babysitting, because they worked full-time themselves. Luckily, an acquaintance of a friend suggested that I rent her brother's apartment in Houston, Texas, because he was leaving to go into the military. I could get into his apartment without having to wait to fill out an application. All I had to do was pay the rent and the utilities, which was easy, if I got a job.

It was difficult telling my boss at the radio station, that I would have to leave, but I knew I couldn't make it in the snow with no car, and the baby. I knew that it was just be too much of a hardship, and not safe for a newborn, since I had no support system there, and no friends yet. I thanked him, and to my surprise, he was very understanding. He was one of the nicest people I had ever met, and with a feeling of gratitude, I put my official notice to quit in, so that he could find a replacement. I worked for a couple more months, which were very difficult because I had no car, and the store was quite a distance away from my cabin.

On several occasions, I found myself dropping groceries all over the snow and ice when bags broke, and the people driving by wouldn't even bother to stop and help. At times I wanted to laugh, other times I just wanted to sit down in the snow and cry. When it was time to leave Tahoe, I was mentally ready for it, because I had such a hard time trying to exist without any friends in the area, and I felt like I was treading water in the middle of the ocean alone. I did smile at the beauty of life, memories of the radio station, and the snow falling, as the sun danced across it. The twinkling of the snow seemed to be a signal, that something magical was on the way. I was a fluffy romantic, and even with the optimistic and maternal Wonder Woman thoughts I was having, I stared out the window, and wondered how on earth I would make ends meet. In many ways, I had repeated the patterns of my own parents, albeit accidentally, but I was convinced that times had changed, and things would be different for me, than they were for them. I also knew that not many babies were brought into the world unplanned, and regardless of planning or legitimacy, they are life's greatest miracle. I thought I could handle anything.

I was having visions of my child playing with my little sister and thinking that we could one day have a large family. I had an ideal family scenario, but my circumstances were much more difficult than that. Like the ant and the rubber tree plant, I thought that if I just tried, everything would work out fine.

Houston was very hot, so it was a good thing my bare apartment was at least air-conditioned. Mother P, was my friend's mother, and she was Black (and preferred the term, rather than African American.) I thought it was best to take people as individuals, and out of respect, I thought it was appropriate to ask them how they prefer to be described, in terms of culture or ethnicity. I classify as Caucasian, but I never liked being called White.

When everyone else turned me away, in one of my greatest times of need, Mother P helped me to acquire the essentials that I needed, to have my baby. She let me know she was there for me, and when the time came, she would get me to the hospital. She brought me a newspaper, so that I could look for jobs, and she told me where the bus line was. She had the demeanor of Dr. Maya Angelou, and because she was part of a large family, and just as warm hearted as my Grandma Markle.

I was so tempted to call my other grandmother and tell her that I was having a baby instead of an abortion, and that the amazing woman who helped me was someone that she would call vile racist names.

Mother P, as I called her, was an angel on earth. Her face was very soft and although she was somewhat petite in terms of her height, she had a wise, timeless soul, and she was strong and robustly built, because of all the great Southern cooking she did. I didn't see her every day, but she checked in on me, to make sure it was ok. After she left, I browsed through the job section of the newspaper, and called to set up an interview appointment for a telemarketing job. Conveniently, it was only 5 miles away and directly off the bus line. Thank God for the gift of the gab.

I was hired immediately, and started my boiler room telemarketing job the next day. It was great because I got to sit all day and set appointments for condo time sharing salesmen. I made cold calls in a radio voice, telling people that they had just won a trip to Aruba or free luggage, and that they had to come pick it up. They could have a prize after watching a video. Since I had a pretty good radio voice, the pitch worked. I baited the hook, then threw the line in the water, and the salesmen reeled the customers in. My job only paid eight dollars an hour, but that was enough for me to pay for my basic living expenses. I got a phone hooked up, and a few pieces of basic furniture such as a bed and a table. Miraculously, things seemed to fall into place, and I had whatever I needed, exactly when I needed it. Without being superstitious, I knew that my baby was meant to be, and against all odds. I called my father to tell him what was happening. I felt that he would at least be comforted by the fact that I had a job, so it wouldn't be as though I was throwing myself and a baby onto the family as a burden.

My reluctance was probably unjustified because, after all, my grandparents helped my mother and father out when I was born, and we became a jiffy pop family, so I expected him to cut me some slack. There wasn't a lot that Dad could do to help me, because I was in Texas, and they were in California. I would have gone back to L.A. from Tahoe, but I didn't want to be a burden. It was very challenging because we had so many miles in between us, and we weren't wealthy enough that Dad could just drop everything and come to my rescue.

I knew I had to get back to California as soon as possible. I still had to get in contact with my daughter's father. In the hot sun every morning, I walked about a mile to a bus stop, and had to wait in the sun for the bus that would take me to my job. Once I was on the bus, it was about 5 miles to the stop. When I got off the bus, I only had to walk a couple of blocks to the very tall, mirrored glass building I worked in. I read that pregnancy and childbirth could be triggering stressors that bring on a myriad of MS symptoms, but I couldn't let anything stand in my way.

As my stomach grew bigger, it was painful to walk to the bus stop, but I had no choice. I learned to adapt, and discovered that I was really resilient, and motherhood also produces a lot of strength. When the big day came, I could proudly say that after 16 1/2 hours of labor, I was more overjoyed at that pain, than anything I had ever felt. My daughter was almost 9 pounds. I had been eating the best ice cream I had ever had in my life, and of course a healthy well-balanced diet with vegetables and lean protein consisting of mostly chicken and fish. I was not overweight, but both my daughter and I were definitely healthy. I just smiled and cried for at least an hour. I knew I couldn't stay in Texas because the telemarketing job would not provide me with enough money to support a child.

Although money is not everything, it's really important for the security of children. Good daycare is not free. I could make a go of things and rough it, but I didn't feel it was fair to put my child through hard times. I had to try to include her father in her well-being. Chris was charmed when he got to see pictures of his daughter, so I went back to Los Angeles with my daughter, and we decided to give being a family a chance.

I would do whatever it took to give my daughter the best life she could have. I remembered what my grandmothers experienced, and what I experienced being with babysitters as a child, and I dreaded the idea of being a single mother, unable to give my child anything less than a charmed life and amazing security. My sister wasn't really left with babysitters that I ever saw, and I felt it was best for a child to be with a family member if a parent had to work. Dad and Doria had made it that way for Meg, but they also had a lot more money than I did.

My grandparents' first home in Newport, Pennsylvania, 1941
(in my family photo album courtesy of Doris Markle)

Gordon A. Markle, Hickman Field Hawaii, 1941
(in my family photo album, Courtesy of Gordon Markle)

Doris Markle and Thomas. Markle - Newport P.A, 1945
(in my photo album, Courtesy of Thomas Markle)

Thomas Markle, 1962 - Newport Pennsylvania
(courtesy of Thomas Markle, Sr.)

Tom Markle and Andy Romanoff, WTTW TV - Chicago, Illinois, 1962,
(Courtesy of Andy Romanoff)

Me, Chicago Illinois, 1965
(in my childhood photo album courtesy of Thomas W. Markle, Sr.)

My brother Tom, - Chicago, Illinois - 1966
(In my family photo album, courtesy of Thomas W. Markle Sr.)

My first grade classroom picture. (Me top row, Second from the left)
- Chicago Illinois, 1971

Me, Grandma Loveless, and Tom - Chicago, Illinois, - Christmas,1972
(in my childhood photo album courtesy of Thomas W. Markle, Sr.)

Dad, Tom, Me, Roslyn – Pennsylvania, 1972
(in my childhood photo album courtesy of Thomas Markle Sr.)
The Adventures of Huckleberry Finn

Me in Gettysburg Pennsylvania, 1973
(in my childhood photo album courtesy of Thomas W. Markle, Sr.)

Me, Dad, and Tom - Newport PA, 1972
(In my photo album courtesy of Doris Markle)

Me and Dad - Santa Monica California, 1978
(in my childhood family photo album Courtesy of Thomas W. Markle)

Left to right: Tommy, Satay, Gail, Gail's sister and Me - San Bernardino California, 1977
(in my childhood family photo album courtesy of Thomas W. Markle, Sr.)

Our house in Woodland Hills, California
(in my photo album, Photo taken by me)

My brother Tom - Woodland Hills California, 1979,
(in my family photo album courtesy of Thomas W Markle Sr.)

Doria and Dad at their wedding - Los Angeles California, 1979
(in my family photo album courtesy of Thomas W. Markle Sr.)

Tom in Woodland Hills California,1980
(In my childhood photo album. Photo courtesy of Thomas Markle, Sr.)

Me, 1980 - Dan Rico Salon, Studio City California
(Courtesy of Glen Wexler Studio)

Azita and me - Westwood, California, 1980
(in my photo album courtesy of Azita)

Me and "Bo" - Woodland Hills, California - 1981
(in my family photo album courtesy of Thomas W. Markle Sr.)

Meghan "Flower" and Dad - Woodland Hills, California, August 1981
(in my family photo album courtesy of Thomas W. Markle, Sr.)

Me and Meg, in our backyard - Woodland Hills, California - 1982
(In my family photo album courtesy of Thomas W. Markle, Sr.)

Meg and Me, in our backyard Woodland Hills California 1982
(in my family photo album courtesy of Thomas W. Markle, Sr.)

My Reuge music box
(photo taken by me)

My all-time favorite picture of Meg with me, at my apartment in Westwood, California - 1984
(in my family photo album courtesy of Thomas W. Markle, Sr.)

Meg and me, my apartment – Westwood, California - 1984
(in my family photo album courtesy of Thomas W. Markle, Sr.)

Meg - Los Angeles California, 1984
(in my family photo album courtesy of Thomas W Markle, Sr.)

Grandma Loveless and Ashleigh, 1986
(in my family Photo album courtesy of Christopher Hale, Sr.)

Grandma Markle and Ashleigh, at Doria's apartment - Los Angeles, California - 1986
(in my family photo album courtesy of Thomas W Markle, Sr.)

Me and my son Christopher - Los Angeles, California, 1987
(in my family photo album Photo courtesy of Christopher Hale Sr.).

Me and Christopher - Disneyland, 1987
(courtesy of Christopher Hale, Sr.)

**Christopher and Ashleigh playing at Grandma and Grandpa's house,
Palos Verdes – California, 1987**
(in my family photo album courtesy of Christopher Hale, Sr.)

"Dad's place" - Vista Delmar Ave., Los Angeles, CA.
(Photo taken by me)

Me and Meg - Vista Delmar house, Los Angeles, California - 1988
(in my family photo album courtesy of Thomas W. Markle, Sr.)

Me in Los Angeles, California - 1989
(courtesy of Leslie Whitlock, in my photo album)

Dad and Meg at the Alamo, Texas – 1992 - photo taken by a tourist with Dad's camera
(courtesy of Thomas W Markle, Sr.)

Wesley, Betty, Me, Meg, Dad – Gloucester, Virginia - 1990
(in my family photo album courtesy of Michael Gosling)

Michael Gosling, Me, and Meg - 1990, Gloucester, Virginia
(in my family photo album courtesy of Betty Gosling)

Meg and Dad, Big Bear Lake – California, 1990
(photo courtesy of Thomas W. Markle, Sr.)

**Meg, Tyler, Dad, Thomas James, and me - Woodland Hills,
California, 1991**
(in my family photo album courtesy of Thomas W Markle)

My beautiful daughter Noel - Albuquerque, NM – 1999
(photo taken by me)

Noel, Me, Dad - Albuquerque, NM - 1999
(photo taken by me)

Meg and Dad at graduation - Immaculate Heart High School, 1999
(in my photo album courtesy of Thomas W. Markle, Sr.)

Noel's 3rd birthday, (Left to right) Annalise Smith, Melissa Smith, Me, Noel Chuck E. Cheese - Albuquerque, N.M - 2000
(photo taken by a customer with my camera)

Me and beautiful Noel, 2006
(photo taken by me)

Noel (off camera) Me, Meg – Albuquerque, New Mexico - 2008
(Photo taken by Thomas W. Markle, Sr.)

Dad, Me, Meg at my college graduation - Albuquerque, NM - 2008
(in my family photo album courtesy of Thomas Markle)

Meg and Dad at her wedding to Trevor – Jamaica, 2011
(my family photo album courtesy of Thomas W Markle, Sr.)

Me and my daughter Noel, on the side of my film shoot,
Albuquerque, New Mexico - 2014
(in my family photo album)

Me with actor Raoul Trujillo, on the set of my film teaser for
***"Angel's Redemption"* – Albuquerque, New Mexico - 2014**
(Photo taken by Mark Phillips)

The Sun UK, 2016
(Photo taken by me at the grocery store, Silver springs, Florida)

Meg and Prince Harry of Wales – London, England – May, 2018
(1114019831 Photo courtesy of shutter stock photos)

Me, and Host Dominik Maur of RTL, Germany – May, 2017
(Photo courtesy of Mark Phillips)

CHAPTER TWENTY

My Jiffy Pop Family

When I got back to California, I stayed in Chris' upstairs Bungalow studio apartment in Venice. It was very small so it wasn't long before we moved into a nice, second story apartment in West Los Angeles. Chris' brother lived below us on the first floor, and was always busy studying for the California bar exam to be an attorney. Uncle Matt was very funny and, kind, even though he had a huge study load every night. He always reminded me of a Kennedy.

Chris and I got married at the courthouse, and we didn't have a regular wedding, because everybody was working with different schedules, and it just would've been chaos for all of us, so we decided to make it simple. Our first year together was very nice; he was romantic, and we made each other laugh. His temper seemed to have subsided, and I really believed we could make a marriage work. It wasn't long before we had our son Christopher. The marriage seemed to be going as perfectly as a fairy tale.

I started thinking about the old saying —If things seem too good to be true, they probably are. Chris was doing very well as a chef's apprentice at a five-star restaurant, in the Century City, which was great for me, because I became a very good cook and developed exquisite taste in food and wine. It also seemed like he was sincere about being diligent and supporting the family. I had so much fun being a mom, that I never doubted myself, or the possibility of being disabled, because I was healthy and happy. Children are the best part of life.

I stayed home with the kids, but several times a week, I would go in to work as a receptionist for a law firm in the Century Plaza

Towers, and my mother-in-law would either come to our house, or the kids would stay at her house, until I could pick them up after work. It seemed as though everyone in both sides of the family was making an effort to unify. I would take the kids over to visit with Dad and Meg, and a couple of times, we even went to Doria's house.

My mother's mother came out to visit us from Albuquerque. It was heartwarming to see everyone happy and I only hoped that it would continue, especially for the children. When she saw my daughter, I saw the look in her eyes, and I knew she felt badly about telling me to get an abortion when I was pregnant. I forgave her. I knew that forgiveness requires the ability to forgive others. Although I struggled with emotions over it, I felt that if I expected at times to be forgiven by others, that I had to forgive others, where reasonable. I could see remorse in her eyes that I had never seen. I could see love, and it was divine.

Grandma Markle and her companion Tony also visited with us, and we all went to Doria's apartment. I wanted my grandmothers to have a larger sense of family before they passed away, and even though the kids were so small, I knew that that was a mile marker in their lives. I knew that those moments created memories that we would all carry with us until the end of our lives. They were beautiful memories. I really wanted that for them. I was happy that both of my grandmothers had the chance to see my kids while they were alive. Even though we could always send photographs, traveling to see each other was difficult because we lived about 1000 miles apart. My grandmothers and other family members were getting older and it was important that they felt a sense of unity in their lives, regarding family.

Ashleigh was too small for Meg to play with her, but it was sweet to see Meg interact with her niece, being so close in age. Meg was too young to understand the concept of the family tree, and what an aunt is, but it was nice seeing them together. I thought I was doing everything right as a mom and a wife, but something didn't feel right. I didn't want to worry anyone in my family, but I really couldn't tell them that my marriage had gone awry. I certainly couldn't talk about my marriage with Meg, because she was too young, and adjusting to Dad and Doria's divorce. I didn't want to try to explain so much to her. I found myself in the situation that reminded me of Grandma Markle saying nothing or candy coating reality, to cope with being unhappy. As much as I said I would always speak out where I felt things were unjust, I was afraid to do it because the kids were so small, and I felt it was wiser to appear as the happy housewife, I tried to keep everything a secret, and see if things would improve. My optimism started waning when my husband started coming home later and later at night. Even though the restaurant where he was working as a chef's apprentice, closed at 11, he wasn't coming home until 4 in the morning.

I drew the line at his assertion that he was spending entire weekends, allegedly yachting with his friends, while I was doing all of the work running the household. I hadn't just fallen off of the turnip truck, and it seemed that there was probably another woman in the picture.

One night, I fell asleep on the couch, waiting for him to come home. Sometime after midnight, I woke to realize what was happening. I taped a note to the front door that said, "The kids are sleeping, please be quiet. Your dinner is cold on the stove, and I want a divorce." Although I was trying to be tough about it, it was a really painful way to feel and to fall asleep. As I lay there, I knew that whatever happened would affect other members of my family. I was worried about how the divorce would even affect my sister, if at all. I felt as though I would be role modeling the message that, when people don't get along, you just divorce. She had experienced that, and I didn't want divorce as a means of conflict resolution to be status quo in our family. Chris and I divorced citing irreconcilable differences. Until we could get our act together, and decide what we wanted to do about making the divorce transition arrangements, it was critical that the kids be in a stress-free environment.

CHAPTER TWENTY-ONE

Bridges

As Dad and Doria finalized their divorce, my life was also transitioning out of what I thought was the perfect life. Divorce is very difficult, but so many people get through it, and I knew I would too. Creating or maintaining bridges between households so that kids don't feel isolated from one of their parents or other family members is sometimes very difficult.

Just as Dad and Doria tried to make their divorce a smooth transition for Meg, I wanted it to be smooth for my kids, too. I spoke to Grandma Markle on the phone every weekend, and she reiterated the fact that "You should get an education, because it is something that no one can take away from you." I kept that in mind, and knew that I could go to school later, but I wasn't ready to do it. I was driven by the perception of limited time and disability, so I wanted to experience more of life rather than being what I considered as sand bagged by school.

My grandmother understood my limited schedule, but still encouraged me to go to college at some point in the future. Women didn't have a lot of options before the 1970s, and I knew that she wanted Meg and I to have a better life than she did. I started to pick up print jobs as a model, but the money was never enough to buy a house and settle down. I would regularly go visit the kids, and knew I wasn't making enough money yet to give them what I felt they should have.

My father-in-law discussed moving his business to Virginia and suggested that it would be a great place for the kids to live, while Chris and I got our careers going. Neither of us could afford to work and pay nannies, and we didn't trust general babysitters.

The area they were moving to was a beautiful community, away from the smog, and the hustle and bustle of Los Angeles. After I did some research, and looked at my options, I agreed, because I knew that the kids would be in great schools, with the same friends, and teachers for a long time, a safe neighborhood, and with the stability of both male and female parent figures in the household. I wasn't going to gamble with the safety of my children. All things considered, my kids moved with their grandparents to a quiet rural community in Colonial Virginia. As predicted, they were very happy, very stable, doing well in school, and had a perfect life that I had hoped for them. I felt like I already walked through fire once, to have my daughter, and I felt like being away from both of them was the equivalent of walking through fire. Dad and Meg didn't fully understand what I had been through, and why I made the decisions that I did, but Dad agreed with me, that it was good for the children. I also had the agreement of my grandmothers. I tried to simplify it for Meg and told her that the kids would just be with their grandparents, and go to great schools far away. I hoped that everybody would understand someday.

CHAPTER TWENTY-TWO

Grasping for Straws

I rented a quaint little place in Beverly Hills, which provided quick access to my jobs, and it was only 10 minutes away from Dad's house. I visited him and Meg when I was not working, and when they were home.

My place was the guesthouse directly behind a rather large, red brick A- frame home near Wilshire Boulevard. It belonged to a quirky aristocratic Peruvian woman who paraded six Pekingese dogs in front of my door, as a wakeup alarm daily. I heard them barking, and I knew that it was time to start the day, with a cup of espresso or tea. Helena was very eccentric and my first introduction to wealthy European culture. Many of her friends were famous opera singers and aristocrats, so suffice it to say, the atmosphere in the household was never boring. Her favorite hobby was using me as her personal Pygmalion. In her mind, she was a mother figure to all, and she made it a point to critique my etiquette, as she saw fit. I knew that she meant well so I played along and appreciated it. She insisted that, when I held a teacup or an espresso cup, that I always have a saucer under it, that I hold my pinky finger slightly upwards as I sipped it. Some of her etiquette guidelines seemed a bit outdated, as she was perceptually gridlocked in the 1950's.

Quite often, her friends from around the world would visit, and spend the weekend. Festivities often centered around making exotic foods for her guests, which were traditional in their home countries. Living there was a memorable adventure in international culture sampling. I was going to a nearby health club and running on the beach daily. I wasn't trying to prove anything to anyone else, but I had something to prove to myself. I thought that I could strengthen my legs so much that I could never be disabled. It was my way of coping with the possibility of MS knocking me down at some point. I was feeling rebellious and, unfortunately, I was in denial, and thought I could never be disabled, as if I was exempt because I was in athletic shape. I didn't want to have a wheelchair waiting in the closet because, to my mind, that would be a resignation. I kept going with doubling my intake of ginseng, espresso, and too much exercise as a coping strategy.

I signed with a talent agency in Beverly Hills and began doing more modeling work, and my dad helped me get a little walk on role on *General Hospital*. I was actually there doing extra work when Director Gloria Monty was kind enough to give me a few speaking lines.

I didn't want my sister to see me struggle with the disability issue, and I didn't want my father to feel as though I would ever be a burden to him either. I felt like I was grasping at straws to be successful, to prove to everybody that I could.

The pressure underlying that possibility was overwhelming. I knew that nobody in my family really had the resources to accommodate me if I was disabled, and I thought they would resent me if they had to, so I found myself floundering, in an attempt to make money with a very uncertain future. In so many ways I began ignoring that I ever had my fall, and a possible diagnosis of MS. I had always said, "What doesn't kill you makes you stronger." Whenever I saw Meg, I tried to have fun, and avoid discussing my physical challenges with her. Hearing about disability might scare her, and I was worried about the fact that there is a genetic predisposition to MS. I felt it was important to role model courage, in case Meg or Tom ever encountered it, or any other physical challenge.

Doria had moved into a nice apartment in an upstairs duplex in Los Angeles. It was an older Spanish building that had hardwood floors, very high ceilings. The cats, Brandy and Zander, lived with her. Meg's room was cute and decorated with her *Care Bears*. I enjoyed spending time with her, even though I was older.

I didn't really feel like I was an intruder unless she had friends over. When she was little, Meg was spending half of the week at Dad's house, and the other half of the time at Doria's apartment which seemed ideal, but Meg ended up living most of the time at Dad's, and would see her mom on weekends, and not regularly.

When I asked her how she was, she always said, "I'm good!" Her braids bounced in a delightful way when she was happy. If she did notice the divorce, I assumed that she would voice it, but she didn't, and I really couldn't tell. When I was in her bedroom, Meg was always quick to show me her new things, which were clothes or toys. I often wondered if the divorce was difficult for her and of the toys and the things provided a distraction from how she felt about it. From what I saw, she really enjoyed having two houses with one bridge between them. It is generally very healthy for children to feel that they are loved by both parents and can comfortably navigate in between both households after a divorce.

CHAPTER TWENTY-THREE

Our Different Worlds

I never saw Doria come over to Dad's place. I wondered if she went away somewhere. We were all busy, so I just figured maybe she would pop in someday. The duplex on Vista Del Mar Ave. was an old house that was converted into two separate units. It had a large second story that was accessible through a wrought iron doorway on the right side of the building. Once inside, a narrow black wrought iron spiral staircase wound its way to the second floor. It had an old Hollywood feel about it. Meg's bedroom was in the rear right, and Dad's bedroom was in the rear on the left. The hardwood floors were lightly glazed and spread throughout the entire top floor.

Dad had a soft spot for homeless cats, so he adopted a one legged cat, that had been coming around the house. He named the cat Reject because no one else seemed to want him. He was a medium set, gray Tabby, with his rear right leg missing. It didn't stop him from hobbling around, but it just made him a bit slower. Immediately following the divorce, Meg lived there half of the week, and then from Junior High to High School, she lived on Vista Del Mar Avenue almost full-time with Dad. It was such a quiet little street, that it didn't seem like it was in Hollywood.

It seemed like Meg's world was very abundant in whatever she wanted and needed, and full of so much activity, that it was a wonder she could handle it all in the course of the day. Dad was very easy-going for the most part, and let her decide what she wanted, and how she wanted things to go. Some people would say that is too overpowering for a child, but he really loved her, and felt that he wanted to give her everything that he didn't have when he was small, because his parents didn't make much money. I don't recall ever hearing Dad say no to Meg, about anything, and I couldn't help but wonder what would happen if he did say no. I couldn't help but think that allowing kids to throw blueberries all over the kitchen floor wasn't such a good idea after all.

Meg was becoming more of a little fashionista every day, and she was very cute. I think I told her she was talented and pretty quite often, but because I wasn't really a peer, my compliments seemed to go in one ear and out the other. I could tell that she was very aware of what her peers were doing, and that was very normal for her age, but I got the feeling that she wasn't really aware of how pretty she was, even though she was well liked at school.

I started going on more commercial auditions and was managing a cosmetic counter at a large department store in the Beverly Center. My schedule was tedious but flexible because I was the manager. I arranged my schedule so that I could have the best of both worlds; making good money, and still work in television sometimes. I didn't know where my paths would lead, and I didn't have strong self-esteem. I just faked it really well. I had had it with my short hair, after I went and sat in a little tiny office on Sunset Boulevard for a shampoo commercial.

As I sat in the waiting room, I felt really ridiculous with my boyish short hair, when a supermodel, whose face I was familiar with, walked in with a lion's mane of hair. She looked like a lioness, and by comparison, I looked like an alley cat.

I just sat there wondering why my agent bothered to send me there. I was being as professional as I could, and smiling to mask feeling out of place, as I contemplated how I could get a full head of hair. My kaleidoscope world became much busier and vivid, when one of Dad's friends connected me to a brand new television situation comedy called, *A Different World.*

The show was a spin-off of *The Cosby Show* which centered around the character, Denise Huxtable, and her experiences at Hillman College, which was modeled after an all-Black college. I was offered the opportunity to work as an extra, and as an under five or day player, which usually involved only being seen on camera in the background, as one of the students, or interacting in the background but sometimes speaking a few lines.

It was an insignificant role, but I always said that, "No experience is insignificant" because, in everything, there is something to learn. It wasn't long before I learned a bit more, and I met some fantastic people there who inspired me. I worked on the show for the first two seasons. I had very short dark hair and pale skin and, because of that, I always felt like I stuck out like a sore thumb in the background. I remember wishing I had Meg's fantastic hair, as I sat helping her with homework one day. Meg didn't usually need help with homework, or she didn't ask me, unless it was math. I enjoyed sitting down doing the big sister thing, but it was funny that as much as I thought I knew, I had to look up reference sources for myself, to understand some of the problems. I had to laugh at myself, but I helped as much as I could. I could never understand why Meg was often frustrated by her hair, and wanted it straightened. Being on the television show, and watching women spend hours in the makeup room getting hair extensions, and seeing social responses to women with long hair, made me realize that Meg would one day be the envy of many women, because of her naturally long hair. She didn't even know how pretty her hair was. While Meg was working on math problems, I was trying to calculate how to get my hair grow really long really fast. Meg had the coolest hair, and I knew there was a way I could fake it till I made it, and let my own hair grew out. I thought I would do the Hollywood thing and get extensions.

One morning, I watched as one of the actresses got her hair done on the set. I decided that I wanted hair like she had, and Meg had. I made arrangements to go to the hairstylist's salon in Los Angeles. I had no idea in advance that it would take eight hours, and that it would be extremely uncomfortable, but I was willing to walk through fire to get that hair.

As beautiful as it was, my fake big hair did have disadvantages. It was really heavy on my head when it was wet, and the little wax balls that attached fake hair to multiple strands of my hair at the base of my scalp, were not visible, but could definitely be felt.

"The grass is greener on the other side," and "If something seems too good to be true, it probably is." That week, I booked a little job on an ABC *After School* Special. I was only a day player role, with under five lines. My contention was that, no matter how small the job was, I would spend as much time on sets as I could, be paid to have fun, and learn as much as I could, because someday, I wanted to work behind the camera.

The job only lasted a couple of days, so I was still working on *A Different World*, the rest of the week. I was enjoying getting more male attention with my big hair. I met a young man on the studio lot who took me on a dinner date. At the end of the night, when he went to kiss me goodbye on the cheek, he reached around to the back of my head, and put his hand at the base of my scalp. I knew I was doomed. I could feel all of the blood in my body rush to my toes, because all of the little wax balls at the base of my scalp attached to the clusters of hair would be a dead giveaway, that the hair was not mine. If the look on his face could say just one word, it would be heebie-jeebies. He pulled his hand quickly away from my scalp, and asked in a mortified tone of voice, "What's that?" Horrified and embarrassed, I replied, "I saw one of the actresses on *A Different World* getting her hair done, and I thought it would be fun to get extensions." I felt myself shrinking. He nodded his head awkwardly, but I could tell that my explanation was the nail in my romantic coffin. He nodded his head awkwardly, and I could tell it was a turn off by the way he cringed, as he pulled his hand away from the back of my neck. Unfortunately for me, part of what attracted him to me was the fake big hair. Then when I thought about it, I didn't feel like I lost much because I didn't want a guy who would cringe about things, anyway. I wanted to date a man with at least a modicum of bravery.

Although I had fun with the hair and felt superficially attractive, little did I know that the wax balls don't adhere to Caucasian hair very well and, within a matter of weeks, they started to slip out. I was left with several thinning areas in my fabulous hairdo. The only way I could hide it was to keep it pulled back in a ponytail. I felt like it defeated the whole purpose of having long hair. Well, it wasn't long before I took it out because it was so expensive to maintain, and quite frankly, it felt ridiculous to have wax balls at the base of my scalp. I was not wealthy, but I suppose I could have afforded the regular maintenance of a lion's mane head full of extensions on my budget, if I sacrificed my entire food or rent budget. I was better off just letting my own hair grow out, so I soaked my hair in an entire bottle of hair conditioner, which made the extensions slide off much easier.

In addition to wanting longer hair, I also wanted darker skin, and erroneously believed that I could have it. I spent as much time as I could on the beach, but at one point, I became addicted to tanning beds. I loved getting my skin as dark as I could, and I realized that I was overdoing it. I had heard a rumor about a woman who abused tanning salon time limitations, by going to several salons and she allegedly did damage to her insides. Needless to say, I abruptly stopped going to tanning salons. I thought if I lay my body out in the sun long enough, that my freckles would be like playing connect the dots, and I would just be dark. It didn't really work, so I resigned myself to using high quality self-tanners to avoid being orange.

The show provided me with a very good regular income, especially when we went into overtime for shooting. Several of the people who were also insignificant cast members, or extras, including myself, brought to my attention that some changes were being made, and that it would affect us.

Production changes were underway, and rumor had it that there were to be no more than two white people on camera at any given time. Complaints started to circulate, but I didn't say anything or chime in, because I was only an extra. I enjoyed the show and knew that I would not be on it forever obviously, as an extra, but I would miss the experience, and several people there. A few people suggested that it was reverse discrimination to exclude white people from the show. I was stunned Caucasian extras would be complaining like that, on the grounds that the show was set around an all-Black college, so it never seemed logical that white people would be on camera in most scenes that took place on any campus setting, anyway. Television programming had been very racist for so long, by excluding the Black community, that it seemed as though more multicultural programming was long overdue. Although I was happy to be there, I did feel a bit out of place on camera as one of only a few Caucasian people in the background. I felt like I stuck out like a sore thumb, primarily because my hair was so short, and my skin was too light. One of the regular actresses who was on the show is Caucasian, but she was a regular supporting character. After the white extra cast members were cut, I was watching the show and noticed that the theme was more culturally specific. That was a lot more character exploration into Black culture, which I thought was appropriate and needed in television. What I also really liked about the show was that it portrayed a very upscale modern, Black family, instead of stereotyping Black families as only living in a ghetto, which was part of the problem with social marginalization as a byproduct of media influence. Television seemed dominated by upper-class white families, and it really was time in the 80's to show successful Black families as becoming more of the norm in the United States, and in the world. Being in Southern California as a young woman, and being part of that show, also gave me the false perception that racism was extinct in the United States.

I was in an upper middle class inter-racial family, and I was in a city that was very wealthy, and actors and actresses, and doctors, and professionals I had met who are Black were socially affluent. I had to realize that my experience and my perception of reality regarding the Black community was very limited, given my geographical location. Generalizations about any ethnic group are not accurate or representative, on the grounds that individuals are all very unique.

I never saw racism in Los Angeles, because there was no racially driven social strain in the areas that I lived. Inner city Los Angeles experienced more social problems then I was able to see. I was hoping that my sister would never have to experience racial tension.

In May 1992 civil unrest broke out in South-Central Los Angeles, after judges acquitted a few police officers for excessive use of force during the arrest of Rodney King. Rodney King was severely beaten by 10 police officers with batons as many other cops stood around watching. His injuries were so severe that they included brain damage, broken bones, teeth, as well as fractures to the skull. A mostly Caucasian panel of jurors found the officers not guilty, and just hours after that verdict, violence and rioting were widespread in South-Central Los Angeles.

Over several days, federal troops and the National Guard were able to control the uprising. Although the riots and protests were not near my Dad's house or near Doria's house, Dad decided to pick Meg up from school and whisked her away to Palm Springs for five days, so that she would not have to be exposed to that kind of social conflict and upheaval. Dad was always taking Meg to different places whenever he could.

Dad worked diligently at ensuring that Meg had a healthy understanding of differences in skin color, especially of interracial families. When she was younger, he would take the heads off of Barbie dolls to show her that families come in variety of colors. Mattel didn't make a wheelchair Barbie at that time, but I wished they would have. Toys and playing can help kids to understand physical differences in a relatable way. Our dad was pretty clever to understand that and implement it.

Everything that happened within our family, at her school, and even at the studios, suggested that racial differences were not an issue, so Dad didn't want her to be traumatized by exposure to rioting, as an offshoot of racial tension. Dad was great about giving my sister age- appropriate exposure to some of the hardships in life, while also sheltering her from those that were not appropriate for kids to see, because she might internalize it the wrong way.

CHAPTER TWENTY-FOUR

Crossroads

In 1993 I got called to go audition for a film in North Carolina at Carolco Studios, and I also auditioned for the television show Matlock, while I was there. The movie I auditioned for was a new Brandon Lee movie called *The Crow*. I ended up not getting cast in The Crow as the female lead, but I did get cast in Matlock. Tragically, Brandon Lee died on the set, when a prop gun fired a real bullet and killed him.

I was excited to tell Dad and Meg that I was cast in Matlock, but it was really hard to tell my kids, because they might imagine that I was making tons of money, and question why they weren't living with me. Even though I was making enough money to make a drastic change in their lives, I still couldn't afford a house that was comparable to what they were accustomed to. I felt ashamed that I wasn't successful enough, and even when I was doing OK, I stayed in the shadows and played down my little successes. I didn't want them to feel like I didn't love them enough to buy them a house. I knew they couldn't understand that it was more than just about a house. Even if I had a lot of money, I knew they had developed strong bonds with their grandparents, and with friends at school, and I wasn't willing to selfishly uproot them.

I knew what my Dad felt like when he left us with our mom for a year, so he could go to Los Angeles to get a job at the studios, and would sometimes call just to hear our voices, but say nothing, because he was too ashamed to tell us that he didn't have the big job yet. I knew what that felt like to experience as a parent.

A good friend of mine, who trained and bred quarter horses, lived on a 100-acre ranch in Virginia. They invited me out to the house, and I thought that since I was only a couple of hours away, I would visit my kids. I was elated to see that my kids were doing great in school, and lived in a beautiful home, in a storybook perfect community. I knew when I saw how happy they were that it would be wrong for my husband and I to take them away from it. I knew we couldn't work out our differences and that really the kids were best staying there, rather than being torn between two worlds.

To my surprise, the visit seemed like any normal day, and there was no noticeable anxiety about us missing each other, which was how I wanted it for them. I played with them up in their attic playroom, climbing on a jungle gym, drawing pictures, laughing and playing hide and seek with them, and running around outside in the yard. I was happily exhausted, and it felt as though we had not been apart. Because they had school the next morning, I thought it best to leave that night so as not to interrupt their school week. Saying goodbye was difficult, but we made good use of the last hour with lengthy goodbye hugs.

Upon looking at my sister's perception of divorce, and my children's perception of divorce and their living situation, I came to understand that children really perceive the world around them as adults shape that perception. There was no anxiety about divorce and living with their grandparents, because we didn't make it an issue. It felt normal and right to them. The divorce between my parents was so stressful because my parents were always fighting. How parents handle divorce has everything to do with how children interpret it.

I left feeling that everything was right with the world. Instead of heading straight back to Los Angeles, I called my friend Mike, and decided to stay with him and his family on their horse ranch for a few weeks.

When I told Mike's mom about Dad and Meg, she was delighted. "Well, invite them out here. We would love to meet them!" she said. I called my Dad, and we were overjoyed that he had planned to bring Meg to visit us on the way to Florida to visit Grandma Markle, and Uncle Fred, since Meg had never met them. My brother and I got to spend quality time with her in

Pennsylvania every summer, but my sister never had the opportunity to interact with her in person. I was able to have a nice long talk with my father about my kids and he completely understood. It was unfortunate that Meg and Dad didn't get to spend time with the kids, but we assumed we could make it happen at another time. The Goslings had a couple of horses that had been pastured but were previously trained as racehorses. As I was standing on the balcony, I watched excitedly as Dad and Meg made their way up the long driveway. I couldn't wait to introduce them to everyone and show them around. I wasn't familiar with the South, and I was concerned about Meg and Dad encountering racism when they made the drive. They did not, and had a lovely trip. I had not seen any signs of racism, in spite of stereotype depictions of the South, so I was under the assumption that it was gone.

Betty and Wesley were so excited to meet Dad and Meg, that Betty went to great lengths to make us a fantastic Southern dinner. The Goslings were moderately wealthy, but everything they had they worked very hard for, and they really appreciated the smallest things in life. Their son Michael was charming and very hard working, even though he was an only child and never wanted for anything. He was crisply dressed at all times and wanted for nothing, but he knew the value of hard work through breeding and training Quarter Horses and helping his parents. I was excited at the thought of getting both Dad and Meg on the horses, even though we weren't sure which horses would be calm enough to put them on. They enjoyed walking around the property, which was surrounded by trees in every direction, as far as the eye could see.

The pasture was larger than any pasture, that I had ever seen. In the distance, there were a couple of mild-mannered horses, but I couldn't figure out which horse would be safe enough for Dad or Meg to ride. Dad was discussing the fact that I was on *Matlock*, and told me that he was proud of me for it. It was only a guest starring credit, so I felt awkward talking about it. Betty chimed in enthusiastically and said, "Samantha is going to be a star!" I really didn't want to be a star, and the hype was embarrassing. I was more interested in what the director was doing behind the camera, and I decided there, that I was more interested in being behind the scenes particularly, as a writer. I looked over at Meg, and couldn't help but notice that she looked very uncomfortable. I sensed that she might to be feeling left out, so I quickly changed the subject, and said, "No, Meg is going to be the star!" I knew I would be kicking myself for that later, because I had just given her her way. I didn't understand it then, but maybe one of the problems was everybody gave in to her, when she was displeased with something. I boasted to Betty about how great Meg was at acting, and that she was taking classes. Betty and Wesley really wanted to talk about Andy Griffith and *Matlock*, and I didn't want to be rude, so I discussed a little bit about what happened on the set, and changed the subject to the beauty of some of the old homes in North Carolina. Michael and I decided to break up the monotony of not knowing what else to talk about by taking Meg and Dad outside to see the horses.

I knew that Dad had taken her up to Big Bear Lake, and that they went horseback riding, so I assumed that they would be comfortable on the Gosling's horses. With the exception of Pistol, the other horses were mares and horses that had been pastured for a few years. Even though I knew Meg had been on horses, I still didn't feel safe about her being on Pistol. Earlier in the week, I was riding Pistol in the field, when he stopped abruptly, proceeded to urinate while I was in the saddle on top of him, and said, "Oh come on!"

Like a bat out of hell, Pistol started crow-hopping all over the pasture, which consisted of wild and unsteady motions, a cross between hopping and bucking. I was worried about being thrown and was about to grab the horn of the saddle and dismount, when Mike's father Wesley, came up behind me with a revolver pointed at me, and commanded, "Don't you get off that horse."

He had a wry sense of humor, so I knew he was not going to shoot me, but he was trying to teach me, that if I get off of a horse while it is out of control, I would never gain respect from the horse, and I would likely be unable to ride it again. I stayed in the saddle, and eventually Pistol calmed down, and I was able to continue my ride with his cooperation.

Meg and Dad ended up not getting on Pistol, but we had fun anyway. They got a complete tour of the stables, and I told them of some of the wonderful ghost stories in the area, that had been passed on through families since the Civil War. People who lived in the area, including the Goslings, spoke of seeing a Civil War soldier in the woods. With perfect consistency, many of the locals described the same figure. It gave me the creeps walking around in the woods by myself, but at the same time I was very curious. I never saw the alleged ghost, and neither did Meg or Dad while they were there. All fun comes to an end, and after a few days Dad and Meg had to go back to Los Angeles and I followed soon thereafter. I had a lovely visit with the Goslings, and I knew that my kids were very well-off, happy and safe, so I went back to Los Angeles with a sense of contentment even though I would miss my kids.

CHAPTER TWENTY-FIVE

The Pushy Princess of Vista Del Mar

Being back in Beverly Hills made me feel like I had to jump back into the rat race. I took a regular job managing a large cosmetic counter, because it was regular income, and centrally located.

I wanted the stability for a while, so I put auditioning on the back burner. I was anxious to visit my brother so Meg, Dad and I drove out to see him one morning. Like me, he had gone through an unhappy marriage and divorce, and had two sons, Thomas James and Tyler. The boys were adorable and always great fun to visit with. They were so much smaller than Meg, that she babysat them a couple of times. They lived all the way in the valley and never came to the Vista Delmar house, but it wasn't hard to drive to see them. My guest house in Beverly Hills was quaint, but it was not as close to everything as I preferred. I wanted to be closer to Dad's place on Vista Del Mar Avenue. It was one of those older buildings in Hollywood that was perfectly nestled in a very stylish older neighborhood at the base of Hollywood Hills, and it was close to work for me in Beverly Hills, and also to Hollywood. There was a woman who rented the small studio unit in the back of the house, that was accessible from the sidewalk on the right side of the building. She had a black potbelly pig, and oddly we saw the pig more than we saw her. I knew she wasn't moving anytime soon so I could not rent the back house. I stayed in Beverly Hills and it seemed like my life was just the cycle of getting up, going to work, going to bed. I did that for a year and although I made really good money, I always felt as though there was something missing in my life. I knew that a lot of it had to do with being away from my kids, so I had to stay positive and distract myself.

The following year, as I was looking for a place to move to that was closer to work, Dad said that I could stay in the spare room of his place, while I looked for an apartment. It seemed like it would work out great for a while. Meg's room was situated just off of the dining room, and once inside, there was a doorway that led to a beautiful blue and white tiled art deco bathroom, and a small room adjacent to that bathroom, which was where I slept. I worked late on the television show one night, so when I got in, I tiptoed past Meg, hoping I wouldn't wake her. In the morning, I shuffled groggily into Meg's bathroom. My legs felt like they had cement blocks on them. The bathroom sink was made of beautiful antique porcelain, with silver art deco handles on it. I brought in my toothbrush and toothpaste, turned the water on, and brushed my teeth. From behind me, I was surprised to hear Meg's voice, in a surprising and authoritative tone, uttering, "Babe, could you remember to put the lid on the toothpaste?" I was taken aback, only because it seemed out of character, and most adults put the lid on the toothpaste anyway, so to be reminded of it in advance, struck me as a bit snippy. Even though it felt awkward, I tried to hide my dismay, and excused it away as "It's a good thing she pays attention to detail." I felt that it was her way of letting me know that that was her bathroom, and she didn't want me messing it up. I thought, "Well, the Princess of Vista Del Mar has spoken." Whatever happened to respecting elders? Her tone of voice and demeanor was very reminiscent of Doria's. She was always different when she got back from her mom's house. I felt like some of the changes in her personality were attributable to a bit more than merely growing up. I thought perhaps there was some negative coaching going on. I got the feeling that me staying there was crowding her space. I could certainly understand that because she was young teenager.

I began my search for a place that I could rent in the immediate area. I sensed that Meg was happy knowing that I was finding my own place, and that she could soon have her territory to herself. Dad was working a long shift on *Married with Children*, on this unforgettable January 17th. I was spending the night at his place, and I slept in the guest room. Meg was at her mom's. Her room was tastefully decorated, and her shelves were home to a couple of my music boxes, that she conveniently owned by squatter's rights, even though I had planned when she was little to give her a few of them, when she got older. I put them there when I was in the middle of moving, but Dad said she didn't want to part with them. I knew that if Princess threw a fit, my head would be on a figurative post beside a canal in Venice so, basically, I complied with her conquest of my music boxes. All things considered, I let her keep the music boxes, and I kept my head.

All was still at 4:30 in the morning, and it was pitch black outside. Suddenly, what seemed like a tornado, hoisted up the building, and pulled it to a slant, so much that everything in the house went sliding on the industrial glazed floors. The house was violently shaking, such that glass was also sliding off the shelves, and breaking across the room. Dad was still at the studio, but as I woke up, I couldn't make sense out of anything. I scrambled across the floor in my nightgown, trembling as I tried to get to the spiral staircase, without falling down the stairs. I held onto the railing and slid down more of the stairs than I actually stepped on. When I got to the bottom and opened the inner door, I found myself grabbing the wrought iron security door bars, which felt like jail bars, and as I was screaming for a neighbor, or anyone to help me, I realized that the key to unlock the door, was back up inside, on the floor or on the kitchen counter. One of the neighbors eventually came to the doorway, and tried to calm me down enough, so I could get up the bravado to go back up inside the house and look for the key. With everything shaking, and broken glass everywhere, I felt like I was on the set of a really bad horror movie. I found the key on the kitchen counter, went back down the spiral staircase, and opened the door. Dad showed up about an hour later, and told me what had happened at the studios with the lights, and the equipment swinging overhead. I figured out that we had had an earthquake, but I did not know that it was a 6.7 on the Richter scale, with the epicenter in Northridge.

My brother Tom had an apartment in Northridge, near the Northridge Mall. I knew that area was devastated so I was worried about him too. There were several aftershocks, so I was afraid to go back up inside, but since Dad was with me, I was OK. I asked him if Meg was safe, and he told me that she was safe, as he had called her at Doria's. She would be home in a day or two. It's a good thing there was an earthquake, because I wouldn't want Meg to blame me for all of the disarray in her bedroom. The entire place was a disaster.

Dad and I worked throughout the rest of the day, to put the apartment back in order. We were just really happy that everyone was safe. I called my brother later that day and found out that he was also safe, even though the building he was in was swaying quite a bit and, after he got out of the building, parts of it did collapse. We made it through the earthquake, but it was so traumatizing, that I thought it gave me PTSD. The Beverly Center insisted that all management personnel go into the stores and start putting them back together. Our store manager called us and demanded that we come in and set the store up, if we wanted to keep our jobs. I knew that FEMA had not inspected the I-beams in the building, and it was still having aftershocks, so I refused to go into the building, and quit that job. I knew I wasn't alone in my phobia of going into buildings in Los Angeles after that.

I was afraid to go on elevators because I thought the buildings would shake and crumble. I couldn't find an apartment that I liked, and the only roommate situation I found in the area that seemed like a comfortable situation initially, turned out to be a man who wanted an open-minded female roommate, who would dust the furniture, wearing a French maid outfit to keep his jolly Roger, Jolly. I wasn't having any luck finding a place or a roommate that I was compatible with and I didn't just want to plant myself anywhere.

In 1993 I was lucky enough to be cast in a *Coors Dry* beer commercial. Even though the beer didn't sell for very long, it did help me to pay bills, and I had a lot of fun. Meg expressed that she was happy for me, and oddly I knew that she would be doing her own commercials someday, so at a minimum, I hoped that I was inspiring her. I continued doing small modeling jobs as well as working at my normal job to keep busy as I regularly checked for apartments that I liked.

CHAPTER TWENTY-SIX

Growing, Growing, Gone

It must've been divine, jolly intervention, because I ended up renting half of the bottom part of the house right below Dad and Meg. Work was only five minutes away for me, and I really liked being closer and towards Hollywood in the Hollywood Hills. We were about a half an hour away from my brother, so we didn't get to see him very much. He had an apartment in the Valley, and had now divorced his wife, Tracy. Although he didn't ever come to Vista Delmar, neither did his sons; we went to visit him a couple times. The boys were very small and still at that giggly stage, so it was fun to see them.

Living in the apartment below Dad and Meg was good, because with Dad's late work schedule, and with Meg's busy Jr. High School schedule at Immaculate Heart, and her friends wanting to hang out, I could be there if they needed help, but I wouldn't have to worry about stepping on Meg's toes. If I came home late, I would not disturb them either. It seemed like the ideal situation.

I never saw Doria come to the house, so I knew that I wouldn't have to be in the middle of any drama. There were some things that I really liked about Doria, but others I didn't. The list of things I didn't like about her was longer than the list of things I did.

I always thought that my sister would become more like my father, but it seemed that with each passing day, she was becoming more like her mother. I couldn't pinpoint it, but something about my sister's tone of voice conveyed resentment, and I wondered if her mother had anything to do with it. Meg liked her room and space very orderly, which was appropriate for a young lady, and the areas outside of her room tended to be less orderly, because Dad would come in, and set things down during his busy work schedule and, that being said, the house was not always perfectly tidy. I would sometimes walk around and tidy things up but made sure not to disturb Dad's things or Meg's. The dining room was lovely, with hardwood floors, and a beautiful China cabinet sat just across from the dining room table. The table ended up being the temporary setting place for a lot of things. Not much life centered around the living room, unless there was company, but we tended to gather in the dining room or the kitchen.

The dining room was well-suited to holiday festivities, but those were usually spent at Doria's house, or at her mother Jeanette's house, and we went to Sandy's and Joe's house one holiday. One morning near Christmas, as we were in Meg's room contemplating gifts, Dad walked in and, in his casual way, looked at us both and threw a catalog on the bed. He said "Here, you guys pick out what you want. " Both Meg and I raised our eyebrows and smiled in curious agreement. Normally Dad would get us something and wrap it, but he thought it might be fun if we just pick out what we wanted. I tried to order something moderately priced out of respect. The catalog was filled with holiday shopping merchandise, including everything from household goods to jewelry and skin care products. It seemed somewhat tacky to jump straight to the jewelry section, but we did. Both of us pointed at several things that were pretty, but they seemed a bit pricey. I pointed at a ring that was about three-hundred dollars. I thought it was reasonable. "This looks nice, it's Tanzanite and 14 karat gold," I said. I thought she would think it's not cool because teenagers like mood rings, and other wild jewelry. I was waiting for her head to spin and splatter pea soup all over the walls, because she turned pale, and I could see her forehead bead with perspiration, as she said in the tone of voice that could have burned a hole in the wall, and without ever even bringing her lips together, "You're not getting that ring, Babe!" Her response made it clear that she was jealous at me picking out something slightly above what is considered moderately priced. I was showing it to her as a suggestion for her, but it went right over her head. I was irritated with her response but I gave in and just said, "Oh I'll just find a cool perfume." I was trying to be fair, but I should have made it clear that it was not about competition, and we could get whatever we each wanted for Christmas. Hindsight is always 20/20.

I handed her the catalog and said, "Why don't you get something you really like?" She smiled and started looking through the pages of dazzling gifts. In jest, I was anticipating that any second, my adorable little sister would go from having a peachy sweet angelic face, to looking like a crazed cat, with a bird in its mouth. To distract from the awkwardness of that moment, I started pointing to things, and suggesting that they would look great on her. I couldn't understand where her feelings were coming from and wondered if her mother had been influencing her. I knew her friends at school were nice girls, so it was hard to pinpoint where that attitude came from, out of the blue. Whatever the case was, I didn't want her to feel bad, so I ignored it. When I compared that moment to the incident in the bathroom about the toothpaste cap, although I didn't want to look too far into it, it seemed as though she was really needing a sense of importance. Meg's words lingered with me though because she seemed to harbor a sense of competition, and adamantly did not want me to pick out a nice gift. It wasn't just that she didn't want me to have a nice ring, it seemed that she didn't want Dad to get me a nice ring. Dad was trying to make us all happy, and he had to wear a lot of hats in his balancing act. We tried to create a family environment, but it didn't seem like Doria wanted to participate, except on the holidays. We were not very codependent people though, and so I tried to mind my own business, and be supportive, and realize that she had things going on in her life, even though it all seemed so mysterious. I tried not to talk about divorce related issues in front of Meg. Even then I knew it was inappropriate for Meg to be put in the middle of adult attitudes being thrown around, which would jeopardize her identity and relationships with everyone. While we were tiptoeing around trying to be considerate, I didn't think Doria was. Something about the idea of our blended family lasting, and the way I hoped things would be. I should've listened carefully when we were at our house in Woodland Hills, and she mentioned the name of her company as being The Three Cherubs, rather than The Five Cherubs, which would have appropriately included my brother and I, since she moved into our lives. While my brother and I were accepting her as family, thinking that there was a future and a normal family life together, we were apparently mistaken. I decided that I would be patient and see what happened. Things never got better. Meg was my sister, and I figured I could have a normal sisterly relationship with her, apart from any relationship with Doria. I knew then, that if she grew up to be like her mom, we probably wouldn't get along. I was hopeful though that she would be her own person, and we could maintain a bond.

CHAPTER TWENTY-SEVEN

Shadows Across the fold in the Road

After the Northridge earthquake, I wanted to find another job that wasn't in a large building such as a shopping mall. I also thought it was time that I use my education in broadcasting, so I took a job at a radio station as morning news announcer and morning show sidekick. It was my first experience with the fact that, even though I was in charge of writing my newscast and choosing the stories that I thought were relevant for my listeners, I learned the hard way that not everybody wants an up ending. My idea was starting the morning drive with a positive story and ending with a positive story.

The O.J. Simpson trial was at the top of the news. I was talking about it so many times throughout my week, that it seemed depressing, and I didn't think he was guilty, so I was feeling an ethical conflict, because of the way it appeared that the media was spinning the facts of the case as they were revealed. I was seeing evidence that did not fit, in my opinion, because I knew the Brentwood area very well.

I was one of the people who felt that racism was a factor in the case, and that O.J. was framed. I think that, like most listeners around the country, it was easy to get vicariously involved with the story. I was learning that people like sensationalism, even when it is gruesome. I did not agree that the story should be at the top of every newscast. I wanted my breaks to start and end on a positive note. Without announcing the changes in advance, I flew the story out the way I thought it should go, just to see what listeners thought. The station general manager walked in, looking like he just jumped off of the cover of the Rolling Stone magazine.

He cocked his head sideways, and said, "Just remember this—If it bleeds it leads." Although I respected his position as my boss, and his vision for the station, I didn't want to be pushing doom and gloom onto my listeners right at the top of the morning commute. After several discussions of the subject and careful consideration, I put in my notice, and I parted with the station on professional terms. Although it was a good experience, I wanted something different. I was feeling like I wanted more in my life, and I definitely wanted to go back to school. I had a couple of friends pulling me in the direction of cross training in the Air Force Air National Guard, and for the Sheriff's Department. I also thought at some point, I could also use my experience in broadcasting, while in the military.

Like my uncles, it was an honor that I wanted to be a part of. I was in great physical shape and thought I could make a contribution by helping others. That being said, I had a long discussion with my father, who was really encouraging and told me to follow my heart and do what I thought was best. I knew that I could get a great education, travel, and help others. I had passed all of my physical exams with flying colors, so I really thought that the doctors I saw when I was much younger were quacks, because I was so athletic. I set out to prove to my family, including Meg and my kids, that I wasn't limited by the possibility of disability, and that in life we could do whatever we set out to do. Meg was in High School, and I thought it really important to roll model strength. I remembered Eleanor Roosevelt saying, "You must do the things you think you cannot do." In hindsight, I realized that I was overcompensating and subconsciously, I was out to show the world that I wouldn't be stopped by a diagnosis. I scored well on my entrance exams and decided to give the Air Force my all. Under the scorching sun of Texas, I was on a run with some fellow airmen, and my right foot began to drop. I didn't know what was wrong because I was in top shape. I was running a five-minute mile and had trained extensively to get to that point. So the airmen on each side of me, put my arms over their shoulders, and helped me get over the finish line. I went to an Air Force neurologist, who after an extensive physical examination and looking in my optic nerve, determined that I was possibly dealing with MS, albeit a mild variant. I was so disappointed that everything I had worked so hard for seemed to be taken away from me. I was honorably discharged and felt that I had to adapt and overcome that, like anything else. I knew that at least I tried. It was really frustrating to know that something like this would keep getting in the way of my life. Just when I thought I was getting back up, I felt like I was being knocked down again. As painful as it was, I was glad that my kids weren't having to experience interruptions because of disability with me. I couldn't tell them what I was going through though. I knew I would have to work it out and deal with it as an adult which was a very lonely feeling under the circumstances.

When I got back home, Dad suggested that I ask Doria if she knew of any disability accessible apartments in the Santa Monica/ LA area. She was studying gerontology, and working with some elderly people, so I assumed that she might know of some resources I could check into. I really wanted an apartment in Santa Monica, so I could still be near the beach. I called her, and surprisingly, I felt that we could have a connection that we had never had. I was hoping that she would have a bit of empathy and care enough to be a friend to me. Our conversation seemed to be really positive and, although she said she would check into some things for me, she never called me back. It made no sense to me because she was working towards a degree in gerontology. Although I was not a senior citizen, I certainly thought she could help me find wheelchair accessible apartments. I didn't understand why she would even bother offering to help the first place, if she was not sincere. It was a very strange interaction.

Meg was becoming more independent, and seemingly more like her mother every day. I didn't know how much her mother told her about the disability I was dealing with, but I felt like my stoicism might have been interpreted as not caring or not communicating. I knew she was busy with high school friends and I didn't want my disability or struggles to bring her down so I didn't tell her about them.

It wasn't hard for me to distract myself from disability when I watched some of Meg's plays on video, because Dad recorded them. I thought she was mesmerizing on stage, and that it was definitely her calling. I was so proud of her. Watching her on stage made me realize that little Meg who sat on my lap, and who was so cute as she threw blueberries all over the floor, was growing up and was almost a woman. I loved that she felt brave and beautiful, and that she seemed to be more assertive with each passing year. I only saw her be overly assertive or bossy twice. I was surprised to find out that after all of the hard work my father had put into helping to create amazing productions for Immaculate Heart High School, Meg would be demanding with Dad. The production of *Damn Yankees* relied on him, and because of a disagreement that Meg had with someone, she was insisting that my father walk out on the production. My dad couldn't do that, because he was a professional, he cared about the faculty and staff, and he'd made a commitment. I didn't understand how she couldn't see that, she wouldn't be doing the show without Dad, and there was no sign of gratitude from her whatsoever. Because he would not comply with her, she refused to talk to him for a couple of weeks and went to stay with her mother.

Something changed in her. I knew that teenagers go through personality changes, but I didn't think she would be so mean to our father. At that time, she did a little video with her friends, claiming that she was not getting along with Dad. It's not that they were not getting along, but rather that she had issued an outrageous demand that he quit a production, because she said so. I couldn't believe that she would have such disrespect for our father, when he'd been supportive of everything she did. He was paying for Meg to get a great private school education, and instead of showing gratitude, she was belittling and controlling. It was the first time I saw her throw a fit, when she could not have her way. Dad had no idea that the whole thing was a snapshot of the future.

I was wondering what happened to the positive effects of saying, "Hail Mary. I always felt as though, life is the stage and everything we do, God is watching us." I thought that going to a Catholic all-girls school would be a great place to develop a moral conscience. I was no saint, but I would certainly never issue demands, and ignore people if they did not comply with me. Our grandmother believed that real strength comes from faith, humility, and gratitude. She always said that we grow and become successful largely because others help us along the way. Although my Dad and I were baptized in the Episcopal church, I had never seen the spiritual side of my sister, so it was good to know that she was in a Christian academic environment, and whether or not she chose to be devoted to any one religion, was up to her, but at least she had the exposure. I thought being in a Catholic all-girls school would have a softening effect on her. Personality is not all nature, or nurture, but there were probably influences outside of Dad's reach and school that shaped her personality. My father always went to Sunday school as a kid in Pennsylvania, and I did on and off throughout my life, even though I was never strictly religious.

I wondered why I never saw Doria go to church. It would've been nice if we were a churchgoing family, but even my Dad believed that religion is in the heart, and something very personal, so he didn't force the issue on any of us. I was looking at it all wrong, and assuming that being in a religious environment would increase the likelihood of empathy or compassion. I was trying not to judge her, but it didn't make sense.

CHAPTER TWENTY-EIGHT

Looking for Mr. Right, the Wrong Way

For the most part it seemed as though Meg was conservative and lady like socially. She didn't talk to me about boys, and I didn't pry because of our age difference. I knew that big sisters don't get to hear everything younger teenage sisters do. Similarly, I didn't tell her about my adult experiences socially. It wouldn't be appropriate. I was notorious for looking for Mr. Right, the wrong way so I wasn't qualified to give her advice about boys or men. The idea of finding someone you have a lot in common with wasn't really working for me.

Even though I wanted to walk in the shoes of a big sister, and give her advice about boys, I thought her romantic interests were her business, and something that she would probably prefer to talk to her friends about. It was not that I didn't care, I just didn't want to be nosy or inappropriate. When I was a teenager, I wouldn't want a sister who was 16 years older than me butting in all the time. I knew that when she wanted to talk to me, she would as it was appropriate. Nikki was her best friend, and girl talk was between them. I understood, because when I was in high school, I would never talk to my parents or older relatives about details of my social life.

I never got to meet Meg's boyfriend, but I knew that he was a very good friend to her, and High School could be a very challenging time, so suffice it to say, we've all heard the saying, boys will be boys, and I was just glad that she was in the hands of a complete gentleman. Dad was very fond of him, so that was a good sign. Dads are often hard to impress when it comes to dating. Even though I was too old perhaps for her to feel that she could relate to me or confide in me, I loved her, and wanted her to spread her wings, and be happy. I thought she would naturally outgrow what seemed like the beginning of having control issues. Pushing margins and learning how to interact with others is a normal part of growing up.

I didn't think Meg really knew how great and blessed her life was, but I hoped that she would, someday. She had the best of everything from the first day of her life on, and Dad paid for most of it. It didn't really matter who paid for it, but Dad was passionate about giving her everything she wanted and needed.

For her own strength and insight, it was important to Dad that she understand how blessed we were, compared to so many people around the world. Just as Dad had taken me to look at the poor part of Hollywood, to emphasize the idea that all that glitters is not gold, he also wanted Meg to see some of the harsh realities of life, so that she would be well grounded, understand reality, and hopefully be grateful for what she had. Upon Dad's suggestion, she went to a soup kitchen as part of a class project. I assumed that she understood that some people have very little, or nothing.

It seemed like she knew that she would never have to worry about money or material things. We were secure and very fortunate to have a dad who would give us anything we needed. That was not a bad thing necessarily, but it's good to have a plan B, and the strength to adjust to a crisis. My motto was always adapt and overcome, but that also included helping others along during a crisis. I was hoping Meg would marry someone like Dad. Since time was passing so quickly, I wondered if she would marry her high school sweetheart, or if she would meet her dream man, in an acting class. I was just hoping she wouldn't meet her Mr. Right in a nightclub. I dabbled in going out with friends past my 10:30 curfew before I had my fall, and I thought I knew what the whole teenage scene was all about. I thought she was lucky to be at a good school, where she met a nice guy, whom she had a lot in common with, and that the picket fence would follow.

I got married in 1997 and had a child in 1998. Time was going by so fast and I was happy, in spite of MS. After being honorably discharged from the Air Force, I felt as though I had to have a family before disability struck. I felt as though I had to hurry and get married, if I was to have another child before the onset of disability again, I didn't do my homework before I accepted the proposal.

I was optimistic that I was making the right decisions, and that I just had to try to adapt to whatever came my way, stay in school, and enjoy being a mom. Dad visited with me and met my baby daughter for the first time. He seemed to enjoy being Grandpa again. I was getting older and felt equipped to give my daughter everything I couldn't give my first kids, by getting my degree and not relying on a man. I thought my grandmothers' fears and concerns ran parallel to my life. My grandmother's words gave me a lot of strength, and I decided to focus on education so that I would never have to feel like a man could walk out of my life and leave me and a child with nothing. In spite of disability, I was going to complete my degree. I decided to get my bachelor's degree in criminology psychology. Because I went to school later in my life, I was going to school on grants and scholarships, but luckily Dad would pay for Meg's housing and tuition. I knew that college life would open so many doors for Meg and I was sure that she would be grateful to Dad at one point, when she realized everything that he made happen for her.

Dad was putting everything in place after her High School graduation, so that Meg would be qualified to associate with people and go places that would make her life whatever she wanted it to be. Meg and I spoke on the phone whenever we could, and I was really proud of her for doing well in school. She was also busy with her friends and social life, and I was busy being a mom, and in school myself. Because of the emphasis on school, our grandmother was proud of both of us.

I often wished that Meg and I were closer in age, as I might have been able to give her sisterly advice, especially in high school. I always second-guessed myself and wondered if she thought the same thing, or if she wanted advice from me at all, but the burden was also on her to express it, if she wanted us to

178   *Samantha Markle*

spend more time together. I just wanted her to know that I was there without any pressure.

I was having a difficult time physically, but really wanted to go to her graduation. Dad went to Meg's graduation and took lots of pictures. I thought my big little sister looked beautiful. I wanted her to do a lot of the things that I was unable to do, as I struggled with disability on and off. Dad paid for Meg to have an apartment, and her independence, until she went off to college. Picking out a college for her to go to was really exciting for Dad. They decided on Northwestern University, because it had such a great theatre program, and it was $250,000 per year, excluding housing costs, which he also paid. Dad would do anything to give Meg the best possible education, as he had done since her first day in kindergarten at The Little Red School House. Dad and Meg took the trip to Illinois to Northwestern University to find Meg an apartment there, which he paid for, and to familiarize her with the campus. Education was a big deal to a grandmother, and she would've been so proud to see Dad take the trip and put Meg in a great University. The more I thought about what my grandmother always said, I realized it was very true. "Education is something no one can take away from you, and with it, you can always find some kind of job."

My daughter was getting bigger and doing well in her little school. Because I had such great exposure to education, I had enrolled her in a Montessori school, that I paid for because I wanted her to get the best possible education that I could afford and, at the same time, I was in school during the day, while she was at her little Montessori preschool. My daughter met some of her first friends there. I was paying for her schooling with no help from my husband. It was a difficult couple of years, but it was a lot of fun and very well worth it. I was lucky to have my wheelchair accessible van that worked very well to get us both around to school and wherever else we needed to go. I took classes while she was in school so I could make sure that I could have my day finished by the time her school bell rang, so that she would never worry. I felt that no matter what I would give my third child the things that I could never give my first children. I had the fortune of having good friends, who also had children that Noel could play with.

I didn't want my daughter to be left with any babysitters either, so my school classes conveniently worked out perfectly so that I could be home for the rest of the day. I got our schedules perfectly synchronized.

If we would have wanted to go to college when young, my father would have provided the tuition for both my brother and me. Nonetheless, my brother and I were never deprived, although at times my brother expressed that he thought it was unfair that my sister got to go to college paid for by Dad. The fact that my brother did not go to college was his own choice. My father was always there for my brother, making his truck payments, helping him with anything he needed, especially money. I was going to school on grants and scholarships, because I was an adult when I went back to school. I made good enough grades, so scholarships were available. Because of my fall, I didn't go to college when I was younger, and I also didn't have the discipline or the focus when I was younger to be successful in college. Better late than never, I suppose. I was happy that my sister decided to go to college straight after high school. Dad made too much money for Meg to qualify for grants and scholarships, so he happily paid her tuition, and all of her expenses.

When I asked Meg what she was going to be majoring in, she was excited to tell me that it was drama and foreign relations. I was glad to hear that because, I knew that if things didn't pan out for her as an actress, foreign relations could point her in a socially useful direction. Dad paid for the internship, but then Uncle Mike having worked for the State Department, gave her a recommendation, which could open many doors for her, if she went beyond the one-month program.

Grandma Markle believed in lifting people up, and she gave of herself so unselfishly, so I thought my sister would have the same giving spirit. I once thought I could see her working as a missionary, or for UNICEF, early in her life.

Dad had once suggested that Meg speak out about inequality, and write the letter that she did to Gloria Allred and Hillary

Clinton, to change the fact that commercials seemed to unfairly portray women as belonging in the kitchen doing dishes, in most advertising. Yes, she had to write the letter, and think about the subject matter, but Dad made the suggestion and planted the seed.

It was really our grandmother who inspired us to go to school, and that had a trickledown effect, because I shared her words of inspiration about school, with my daughter about school, and my daughter was a very good student. I was fascinated by her zest for learning. She adored science and animals, so I could envision her becoming a veterinarian or whatever she chose to be when she grew up. It was a good thing she was so focused on school because her father and I were going through a horrible divorce. I had already experienced a divorce in my life when I was younger, and I knew the importance of trying to make it as smoothly as possible for children. I was granted physical custody of my daughter, and in the beginning my ex-husband got supervised visitation, until he would be able to see her every other weekend. We shared legal custody of our daughter, but the goal was to create a bridge between two households just as Meg had with Dad and Doria. It was very challenging to be a single mother, handle school, and disability progressing. The days flew by so quickly and it seemed as though I would pick my daughter up after school, and although it was fun, and I enjoyed every minute with her, there never seemed to be enough time in a day to do all of the things that we wanted to do before bedtime.

Dad wanted to visit my daughter and me, while Meg was getting ready to go to college, and he gave me Meg's graduation photos and showed me the videos. I was looking forward to having my dad there, because my divorce was so difficult, and I was really needing a sense of family emotional support. Instead of flying, Dad wanted to make the trip by car, so he would have to drive all the way from Los Angeles to Albuquerque New Mexico. Meg would not be making the trip with him but she would be coming out when I graduated. I would've liked to have visited with her but, immediately after a divorce, I also didn't want to bum her out. Things were going great in her life. The weather was changing, and it was unpredictable. It was starting to get very cold, but I didn't think it would snow and I certainly didn't think it would snow in the desert of California or Arizona. As we were solidifying plans on the telephone, I repeatedly emphasized the importance of wearing a seatbelt, which seemed silly because he had been driving for so many years. I felt like I was being too much of a worry wart. He assured me that he would be fine and reminded me that we had taken so many road trips from Chicago to Pennsylvania, and that long drives were fun for him.

When it came time for him to leave, the weather was fine in Los Angeles, but he was prepared and had a heavy jacket, because the forecasts said the weather would be getting colder. My daughter and I were really excited and spent time preparing the house and planning what we would do when my dad arrived. We went to the grocery store and we loaded up on food and great snacks, so that she and her grandpa could have a snack party.

Later in the day, I checked the weather and was worried when I found out that there was a huge snowstorm hitting Flagstaff, and Kingman Arizona, and also New Mexico. I was unusually nervous and something just didn't feel right. He said that he would stop and call me when he could. Too many hours had passed without hearing from him and I began to panic. I had horrible thoughts of him sliding off the road, or being stuck in deep snow in the middle of nowhere. There were long stretches of highway in that area, where there was not a gas station or rest stop at the time. Several more hours passed, and I knew I had to call state troopers to see if there had been any accident reported.

I didn't want to panic my daughter, but I was trying to hide tears. I knew something was horribly wrong. I told my daughter that he probably stopped in a hotel to get some sleep because it was such a long drive. The following day he called me and let me know that my suggesting that he wear a seatbelt must've been a premonition because his car flipped in the snow in an embankment and he was suspended upside down in the vehicle. He had a rescue crew get him out, but it took them a while to get to him. I was also worried because he's a big guy, and I thought it would be dangerous for him to be flipped over in a vehicle and hanging upside down in a seatbelt. I was so relieved that he was alive, and thankful that he placated me, and put a seatbelt on.

When he finally arrived at my apartment, I was overjoyed but more than anything I realized how precious life is and how easily and quickly I could have lost my father. I vowed to maintain very regular contact after that. Our visit was a lot of fun, and what struck me as funny was the fact that my dad spoiled my daughter just as he had Meg when she was little, by letting her throw candy wrappers everywhere, eating lots of sweets (when I normally limited sweets to once a week). It was her time to cut loose with Grandpa, and I thought it was wonderful that they had that time together. Noel was proud to show him her artwork and her favorite Breyer horses, and her room was full of them, so show and tell time was lengthy.

Of course the visit wouldn't be complete without toy shopping. After we went out to dinner at a nearby Mexican restaurant, and we went to the mall, we were exhausted. I put up an air bed for Dad in the living room, and we all got a good night's sleep. I wished that he could've stayed a couple more days, but he had to get back to attend to Grandma Markle, and to check on his cat.

When Dad left, I was of course worried, until I knew he made it home safely. I was inundated with writing lengthy papers for school. I just kept chipping away at the block, and I knew that Dad and Meg would be coming out for my graduation, and all of the paper writing would have been worth it.

CHAPTER TWENTY-NINE

The Lady in Blue

I remained diligent at school and so had Meg. I felt as though we had all made my grandmother proud of us. I was looking forward to my graduation and my sister's. Although disability interrupted my education when I was in high school, I was making straight A's in college. Doing homework and writing papers became effortless and sometimes even enjoyable.

I was sitting at my desk writing when the phone rang. I was pleasantly surprised to hear that Meg was calling me during her internship in Argentina. Dad paid a hefty fee for her to participate in the month long program, that Uncle Mike had given her a letter of recommendation for.

The first thing I heard her say was, "Oh my God, Babe! You're not gonna believe this! I'm in the most amazing penthouse that they put me up in, it's like being royalty or something." I was so excited to hear that she was treated well and having a great time, but I was dying of curiosity and wanted to hear more about the handsome men everywhere, and whether or not she had a romantic interest. "So what exactly do you do in your position?" I asked. Enthusiastically, she replied, "Well, Babe, I get to be a go-between for foreign dignitaries and the media here, like a media liaison." I said, "Wow I'm proud of you! You get to spend a whole month doing that! I know you're going to do great, just really be aware of your surroundings, and take a lot of pictures," I said. I knew she couldn't take pictures while she was working, because that would not be professional, but I was hoping she would squeeze a couple in, when she was in the penthouse apartment on her own time. Being there would be relatively easy for her because she was fluent in Spanish as her second language. It was a perfect position for her to be able to interpret between dignitaries, as they interacted with the media in Buenos Aires. I also knew that Dad wouldn't have to worry about anyone taking advantage of her, because she understood what they were saying. Dad made sure that she had plenty of spending money for whatever she wanted, so she didn't have to work while she was doing the internship. It was an important opportunity, and even though it was only for one month., Uncle Mike had worked for the State Department for 40 years, and retired, so his recommendation carried a lot of clout.

Meg had not completed her degree yet, so this experience would go a long way for her resume even if she didn't finish school. Uncle Mike made sure that she was well protected while she was there. All he had to do was put in a couple of phone calls. I heard she was escorted by military security, and no doubt was surrounded by very handsome men, so I was assuming that she would meet her Prince Charming there, and not want to come back to the United States. Sadly, though, amidst all of her excitement, I never heard her express gratitude to Dad or Uncle Mike for the experience, but I figured maybe she would after she got back to the United States, and everything settled down.

Since I was writing at 200-page paper, and I was exhausted, I would have gladly traded places with her, but I doubted she would've wanted to trade places with me. She seemed like she was exhilarated. When she got back to her apartment, I knew that she had just been through a whirlwind experience and the return to Los Angeles would seem boring compared to what she had just experienced. Within a week I got a call from her, and she was feeling somewhat depressed. I had no idea what she could feel that way about, because she just had such an incredible experience.

I was concerned because she didn't seem like herself, and I thought she would call Nikki when she was depressed, rather than me. She's my sister, so I was open to whatever she needed. She said she was having headaches to go with it all. I thought that was probably because of such a contrast between the excitement of being in Argentina and being back in Los Angeles without a lot going on. She didn't tell me if it had anything to do with a relationship or not, and I didn't pry, because I knew that it was her business, and she would tell me whatever she wanted to.

When she said she was feeling depressed, I was a little bit worried. First I wanted to see if I could get her talking. On one hand, I thought she was being a drama queen, and on the other hand, I loved her and thought maybe I could help. That being said, I said, "Are your windows open? She said, "Well my curtains are closed." I replied, "I want you to get up, and go open them." I had never seen her worried because she kept repeating, that she was "depressed." I said, "Listen to what you're saying to yourself." I said," Meg, if a director told you to be happy, and get up and go for a walk outside, would you?" She said, "Of course I would." Her response suggested to me that a lot of what she was feeling was something she could change, and that maybe all she needed was to change her outlook. I said, "Good, then get up and get dressed, and go for a walk, and stop saying you're depressed, and start saying positive things." Sure enough she did it, and later on she let me know she felt a lot better. I couldn't tell if she was only patronizing me, or if it really worked, but I was hoping that I could show her how to change the way she feels by moving around, and by changing her narrative. I wanted to help her, and whether or not she took it seriously was up to her, but I knew she could turn things around if she just focused on it. I thought I knew everything about problem solving, because I was studying psychology and I really wanted to help her. At times I felt like the character Lucy in Charles Schultz' *Peanuts*. I loved giving advice. I tried to strike a balance so I didn't come across as preaching.

I was worried about Meg because she mentioned having headaches. I knew that she had dealt with some mold in her apartment in the walls before, and I wondered if the headaches were like headaches I had with MS. I was hoping that would not be the case. I knew she had to see a doctor about something like that. I didn't want to worry her, so I didn't talk about it.

She seemed to be feeling better soon so, for what it was worth, I thought that I could be helpful over the phone. It seemed like she understood that I was there for her, in whatever capacity I could be. It was a nice interaction, because for the first time in our adult lives, we were seemingly having a real conversation as sisters. It was nice to be able to engage with her at a very human level, even if it was a bit one-sided.

We weren't talking about acting, we weren't talking about money. We were talking about normal everyday life. I wanted her to know that she could call me anytime. I knew there were some things she could not call her friends about, so whatever the case was, I was glad that she called me. I knew that she had friends and other people she relied on or called on for advice, so I respected that space.

Meg met Trevor in 2004, and they became really good friends and because she didn't have a lot to say about it, it made me think she was in a serious relationship. I was just glad she had a male companion who would be protective of her. I had never had that, as my relationships developed too quickly, and that was probably my own mistake. I was always afraid to ruin a good friendship with romance. Hindsight is 2020. I was happy that Meg seemed like she was going about relationships the right way, unlike the women generations before us in my family.

In 2005, my mother's mother died. I looked back on all of my memories with her, and in spite of things I disagreed with, I appreciated what she shared with me of her life. I wondered how much of her life made her happy. I often thought that she would die, bitter and lonely, because she did nothing but work her whole life. I fondly recalled a monumental conversation we had a couple of years back. As we were on the phone, I asked her what she was doing with her day. The clouds parted, and with a smile in her voice, she said, "I am having lunch with my black friend Theresa." This was a mile marker for this woman who was raised out of the depression in the Deep South, and who was always a racist. I knew she felt remorseful about the horrible things she'd said about my friend when I was in first grade. I never thought that she would acknowledge someone with darker skin than hers, as a friend. It signaled to me that she was at peace within herself. I thought that if she could open her heart, and her mind, then anyone could. I wanted to tell Meg about it, but I didn't want to hurt her feelings, by discussing racism, so I left it as a non-issue. I felt uncomfortably sandwiched in between a generation of racial hatred and of embracing diversity. I felt that it was time to let the issue be buried with my grandmother. Although she passed peacefully, I was still a bit sad about her death. I was in need of some good news in the world. Big news came when Meg finally got a regular job that she was excited about, and so was Dad. She was cast as a briefcase girl, on the Hollywood game show *Deal or No Deal*. She started in May of 2006, and even though I didn't see the first episode, Dad told me she did a great job, and I couldn't wait to see the next episode. When I finally watched, I thought Meg looked fantastic, but the first thing I thought was They must've stuffed her bra. I knew there was tape up under there, or something, because she was not that busty. I was wondering if she had a boob job, or if it was just Hollywood magic but it looked great. It just wasn't the Meg that I knew. I spoke with several of my friends who had seen that show, and even though it had not been on that long yet, word was getting around about it. She wasn't making a lot of money, yet I was happy for her, because it was a good start on a resume, and to start making real money.

When it came time for me to graduate, I had accomplished what I thought was impossible.

I finally got my B.A., in Criminology and Psychology. I was elated that Meg and Dad would make the trip to come see me, because we could be together. I just knew that wherever Grandma was in Heaven, if she could see us, she would be proud to know that everything she said to us about getting our education, because no one could ever take it away, would have not been in vain. Trevor stayed in Los Angeles, and Meg and Dad drove to see me, and Meg got to meet my daughter, for my graduation. I drove my daughter in my wheelchair accessible minivan, and Dad and Meg followed behind us, in his Ford Explorer.

When we got to the graduation ballroom, I was so thrilled that I finally did it. It was only a Bachelor's degree, but until people try getting through school in a wheelchair, they have no idea how hard it is. I was suddenly in complete admiration and awe of all the students around the world who completed school, in spite of disabilities.

As we filed into the auditorium, one thing was really obvious and shockingly funny. All of the young men in the auditorium were looking at my sister in her little blue halter top. I thought some of them probably recognized her from Deal or No Deal, but I didn't realize how many people watched that show. I didn't watch TV much. I laughed, because she was so pretty, and she had become more curvy. I felt oddly protective of her, like a little old lady. They stared at her, as if they were hungry wolves. Seeing the looks in their eyes made me realize that my sister had arrived at being a woman. I would never forget the whispering around the auditorium because of the Lady in Blue. After my graduation we went back to my apartment and dad gave Noel and Meg money to go to the mall. It would be a nice time together for my sister and my daughter.

When they got back, I thought about seeing my little sister all grown, up in the same room as my daughter, who seemed to be growing up so fast. I could tell that my father was happy to see three generations of his bloodline in the same room, by the way he just sat on the couch with his arms crossed, grinning. Aside from the happy grandpa grin, he mentioned several times that it was a great feeling for him.

I wondered how long it would be, before we would all go to my sister's wedding, and when my father would be able to see her child or children in the same room with all of us. For me a fairytale life, would be to have all of us in the family together in one room including our children, someday.

CHAPTER THIRTY

The Lady in Red

When Meg got back to Los Angeles, she called me from the Green Room of *Deal or No Deal*, and it was refreshing to hear from her, but I wondered why she was calling me from work. I asked her how things were going, and she said, "OK," but she didn't seem very happy. I could tell that she felt somewhat objectified, because she was in a short red dress, and was made to look busty.

That was part of the appeal of the show, to have beautiful young women in short dresses, especially to appeal to the male audience members. Meg really had a professional attitude, even though it was only a stepping stone to other jobs. She expressed to me that she felt odd, because most of the girls were Maxim models, and she would never insult them, but she knew that she wanted more of an intellectual challenge. I just told her she looked great, and I was proud of her for sticking with it.

I did think they were lucky to have her, because when she smiled and opened a briefcase, she did it with style. She had a contagious smile, and she helped to make the show fun. I could tell that part of that smile had something to do with Trevor. There was an exuberance in her that I had not seen before. I knew they were more romantic than she was letting on, especially since they were traveling together. It seemed like she started to grow up in that relationship, because it was Trevor who opened the windows of the world to her, after Dad built the house and the entire foundation. I knew that Meg was making a fair amount of money working on the show, and it dawned on me that if she had money to travel and have fun with, that maybe she could pay dad a little bit of tuition money back because he was getting up in years and

Northwestern was $250,000 a year. I called her and suggested it, and I had always had a habit of sticking my foot in my mouth, but that was a lulu I was surprised to hear her say, "There are too many cooks in the kitchen, Babe." Meg saying that to me felt like nails on a chalkboard. I didn't think I was being a cook in the kitchen, but I felt qualified to have an opinion and make a suggestion about our father. I didn't think I was any different than anyone else in a family who would discuss parents.

I didn't know why that would upset her so much. I thought she would say "Yeah that's the least I can do. It was an incredible experience, and of course Dad gave it all to me, and now he's retired, so maybe I can help him out in return." Her education cost more than 1 million dollars. I knew that Dad could've put that money to go to use in his old age, but he sacrificed it, and I thought that deserved a little reciprocation, because now he wouldn't have it for himself.

Dad never wanted to be paid back, but I think it was just the principle, because he was retired and although he made decent money in his retirement pay, he still experienced a couple of rough spots, and I thought it would be no big deal for her to help. He had been supporting her all the way up through meeting Trevor.

Dad was also fully supporting Grandma Markle in a rather expensive nursing home, so that she would be safe and comfortable. The bottom line was that Dad gave Meg everything, always, and was self-sacrificing for the family, and I thought the least she could do was be a little bit compassionate in return. She suggested that it wasn't my business, but because he is my Dad also, I thought it was my business, and I was being caring. I could say confidently that that was our first official spat as sisters.

I knew she wasn't eternally mad at me for butting in because, about two weeks later, I got another call from her, and she was in Trevor's bathroom. I knew it must be important if she was calling me from the bathroom. I could hear Trevor's friends laughing in the other room. Curiously and awkwardly I asked, "What are you doing, are you at a party?" She said, "No, I'm in Trevor's bathroom." In an almost adolescent giggle, she chimed, "I'm looking in the medicine cabinet." I was thinking, "OK cut to the chase." And then her voice sounded as though she was mesmerized, as is if she had been looking at the Mona Lisa. With a long drawn out breath, she said, "It's so weird seeing my toothbrush on the shelf in his medicine cabinet." I was thinking it was weird hearing my sister describe being in a man's bathroom. I knew that marriage was coming down the pike. I smiled at the realization that my little sister was having some sort of epiphany, because I knew that she had had boyfriends previously, including in Chicago at Northwestern, but there was something special about her toothbrush in his cabinet, which made her realize that this was serious. Cautiously, I said, "Well, it sounds like you two are happy." She said, "It's incredible, Babe." Apparently the relationship was working very well with her schedule at *Deal or No Deal*, and for the first time in her life, I thought she was settling in to adult reality.

I was happy for her because, I knew that she wasn't using Trevor, and he wasn't using her. They were truly best friends before becoming romantic, and I felt that their love was real. Hollywood can be challenging on relationships because there's so much temptation around, and I felt that she was in a safe and solid relationship that could last forever. Trevor was really Prince Charming, but then again, so was our father. When I really thought about how she treated Dad when she didn't get her way, there was a little part of me that just kept thinking, "Trevor is next."

It was tough at times being an older sister, because I had to remind myself, that there were a lot of things that weren't my business to intervene in, especially with regards to her personal life. I just thought, "She is mature now, and she'll be really good to Trevor. They will probably grow old together." I thought it could be a Hollywood fairy tale.

Meg quit working on Deal in 2007, probably because she was moving on to other things because, as she had expressed, she didn't feel right being there. She knew it wouldn't last forever. I stayed steadfast in school and I felt like I was going to be a professional student forever, because I was stuck in a black hole of paper writing. I knew I only had to go until 2011 for my M.A.

2011 was very big year for our family. Meghan got her big break on the USA network cable TV show *Suits* I graduated with a double Master's degree in Counseling, and Vocational Rehabilitation Counseling. My daughter was an A student, Meg and Trevor got married, and we experienced a tragic loss in the family.

I knew I couldn't go to the wedding, because it was held in Jamaica on the beach, and electric wheelchairs just don't work in sand, and I didn't have anyone to travel with me who could help me. I would need help everywhere, including the airport to the hotel room, and I didn't have a travel aid at the time, and my daughter was in school. I was also doing my counseling internship and practicum. Dad went to the wedding, and my oldest daughter also went. As usual, Dad took a lot of pictures. I had connected my oldest daughter and Meg again because they were close in age. I was delighted that my daughter could feel a sense of our family, outside of my ex-husband's side of the family.

Everyone at the wedding was given a bag of marijuana as a gift bag, which was a common thing in Jamaica. I knew that Doria must've been singing and dancing the entire time. The wedding was really very upscale casual, even though it was on the beach. It seemed like a lot of fun, and I knew from the moment she said, that she couldn't believe her toothbrush was in his cabinet, that this would be the outcome. They had both had come quite a way together, through thick and thin, and Trevor had loved her like no one else, even when she was sick and crabby. Together they progressed in their careers. It really seemed like a match made in Heaven. I could tell it was a proud event for Dad because he poured so much of his heart and soul into Meghan. He could finally see her happy in a long term relationship.

The Lady in Blue at my graduation, had become the Lady in Red on *Deal or No Deal*, and then she was The Lady in White at her wedding to Trevor. I watched her change quite a bit, and although I had never seen her express an interest in religion, I was surprised that she was thinking about it for Trevor. Trevor's family really adored her, and at one point she was considering converting to

Judaism. I thought that was a lovely thing to do, and I was hoping she would go through with it. Grandma Markle couldn't go to the wedding, because it would have been too hard on her, but I knew she idolized Trevor and Meg.

Dad paid a lot of money for Grandma to be in the best nursing home possible, but he couldn't always be there, and so Meg would visit with Trevor, and Grandma developed a huge adoration for him. Every time I spoke to her on the phone, everything she talked about included Trevor's name. It seemed like she was eating sleeping and breathing Trevor.

Sadly, we all watched her cognitive abilities decline, to the extent of hallucinating. She regularly talked about a cat that she didn't really have. She often said, "This darn cat keeps running in between my legs." I didn't want to scare her, or question her mental functioning, so when I spoke to her on the phone, I just agreed with her and said, "He will eventually find a place to go to sleep, Grandma." I even tried to say funny things about cats to get her to laugh. If she was experiencing dementia, I wanted it to be a pleasant experience for her as much as I could help it.

As much as she adored Trevor, there were times when she would speak to me, and she started forgetting his name, and would say, "That very nice fellow was here." It was heartbreaking to see my grandmother slowly slip away. I knew that she had had a very full life, and in her last years, even though my grandfather was not good to her, her companion Tony, took her dancing and traveling, made her laugh, and rebuilt her self-esteem, after my grandfather had broken it down. We all knew that she felt love from the entire family in her last days. I Meg was enjoying her biggest break yet, on *Suits* I had heard that some of the producers involved in the show were Northwestern alumni, and so it seemed as though everything that Dad gave her led her to where she wanted to go in her career. She had to do the work, but the foundation was definitely laid by Dad.

Time seemed to be moving very quickly, and Meg was traveling as the ambassador for *Suits* which made it almost impossible to get a hold of her. I was really worried about Grandma, and sad that I couldn't be there.

On September 5th, I got a call from Dad, and in a very somber voice he said simply, "Your grandmother died." I dropped my head into my hands on my desk and screamed the loudest guttural screen that I could. The pain of my favorite grandmother being gone was indescribable. She died in her sleep. I spent weeks grieving and going through all of the greatest memories about her, and I promised to honor her words, and pass them down in the family. Grandma was proud of both me and Meg for going to college. There was so much more I wanted to say to her. It was so profound to me that in most cases that when someone dies, friends and family are left feeling as though they didn't get to say what they really wanted to say to that person. It made me feel as though, moving forward, I should take some time for each close friend and family member one day, and say "pull up a chair," sit down with them, and say everything that I always wanted to say, so that they could hear it all before they die.

After she died, almost everything I did, I did with her in mind. Since I'd finally graduated with a double Master's degree in counseling, and vocational rehabilitation counseling, I was exhausted from school, because it was such a long haul and all of it, I did in a wheelchair. I had a personal helper/caregiver helping me, and cleaning the house, so it was much easier to get organized, but I didn't have someone with me at school. I couldn't stand independently, so I was having someone help me get dressed, showered, organize my paperwork, and I really felt as though I couldn't have done it without someone assisting me. At times it was humiliating to feel like I needed that, but I felt blessed to be able to have that help. I didn't have to be a burden to family, because I had everything I needed to maximize my quality-of-life, and be able to multitask even though my level of disability was pretty severe. I could not stand, and I began losing strength in my back, and had limited use of my arms. I had lived a very athletic life when I was younger, and I had spent most of my life "seizing the moment," because I knew the day could come when I would deal with more severe disability, so I still felt as though I had planned properly, and I could handle anything. As always, I felt I was racing against time

CHAPTER THIRTY-ONE

Stop the Merry-Go-Round

Meg was doing really well on *Suits* but I couldn't help but wonder how commuting and distance would affect her marriage. I was happy to see that Meg was close to Trevor's family.

In 2013, I could tell there was trouble in paradise because Dad wasn't talking about Meg and Trevor very much, other than to say they were working some things out. I was in shock because I thought they had a marriage that defied all odds in Hollywood. They had something real, and many Hollywood marriages, didn't seem to be based on such long-standing friendships. I thought they could survive anything, whether it was distance or temptation of other attractive people in their circles. I heard from an inside source, that the strain of distance got to be too much, and it wasn't just one-sided. I had a feeling it wasn't just the strain of distance, but rather, if there was someone else in the picture, that it likely had to do with other factors.

We heard through the grapevine that Meg was involved with someone on the show, and I was disappointed to hear it, because Grandma loved Trevor so much. I tried to keep in mind, that since we were not there, we really didn't know. I realized I shouldn't make it a personal thing, and it wasn't really my business. All things considered though, I don't know any family who doesn't talk about how other family members are doing. That's just the way it goes. I wondered if Meg was needing more support from me, but I didn't know what to say, and I also didn't know at the time, that her best friend allegedly got close with Trevor. I could interject my opinion about matters pertaining to my father, but with regards to Trevor, I stayed out of it. A family insider said,

"Babe, don't be so mad at Meg, because Trevor is not blameless. It takes two." My ears were steaming, because I never would have thought about it from that angle. It really does take two to tango. I understood that things are not always as they seem, from the perspective of outsiders. I felt as though she could finally understand what I went through in my marriages. We really didn't talk about her marital problems, and I wish that we could have because I had been through it and felt as though I could be an experienced source of comfort, and maybe advice. She didn't reach out though, so I assumed it was painful and that she wanted to work it out privately. I knew she was busy, but I also realize that I thought about her quite a bit and tried reaching out, but it was not reciprocated and I respected that because I knew she was under a lot of pressure. As women, we were growing and being pulled in very different directions, although we had quite a bit in common. I had always assumed that we would grow together rather than apart. Families don't always grow together.

In April 2015, even though I was in an electric wheelchair, I was so proud that my film script, *Angel's Redemption*, that I had been working on for several years, was moving into development. Before I had development funding, I was working on a shoestring budget, and was lucky to have very talented cast and crew. At that time, I called my father, and let him know that my project was picking up traction, and that I had a location scout already working to find the perfect place to film *Angel's Redemption*. My companion, Mark, acted as an all-around assistant, and even safeguarded the food under the tent, especially the donuts. I co-directed with a wonderful director. I enjoyed teaching my daughter how to be a production assistant, and to apply makeup for film, because I shared with her some of the techniques I learned from Doria, and that I learned watching makeup artists over the years.

Because I was trying to maintain a bridge between our two households, I had my ex-husband work on the set as an armorer. He donated his time, and the project was fun for all of us. There ended up being a drug overdose in the neighborhood that day, on the street next to where we were filming, and the police who responded and blocked the street off, ended up eating all of our donuts, and drinking our cold beverages, but we thanked them for their service. I thought the donuts and beverages were a fair trade for free security on the set. We knew that our set was safe, because it was being occupied by at least 25 police officers. I was going though casting in my mind, because I had not yet hired a casting director. I naturally thought about my sister as a female lead. I asked my father about it because she was working and traveling, at the time, and he thought she might be busy. I thought it might help her be discovered. That was silly of me to think because she was already working. I just wanted her to know I cared, and I thought it would be a great way to bring family together into my project.

My father had agreed to work as the Director of Photography when we started to film. I thought it would be wonderful if Dad, Meg and I, could all work together on a film in his lifetime. In any case, I couldn't wait to tell her about it. I knew she had a lot on her plate between her career, and her divorce from Trevor, but I thought it would be refreshing for her.

I couldn't reach my sister during her divorce, and it was so difficult feeling like I knew I could help her but I couldn't be there for her because she was being really stoic about everything. I was not privy to what was really going on, even though I was hearing about it. I couldn't offer her advice without revealing my source, and I was sworn to secrecy.

I was sitting looking at some of the pictures that Meg sent me from their travels, and I couldn't believe that something so beautiful could vanish. I felt sad because I really wanted that to last forever for her, but there was a barrier that I could not get through, to help her and let her know that I was there for her. I fluctuated in between wondering if maybe I wasn't fabulous enough, because I wasn't a jet setter, or a celebrity, but then I thought maybe she would want the ear of a family member, someone who was down to earth, and not involved in all of that Hollywood stuff, even though I had a project in the works. I was just hoping that she would call me. I was afraid to bring the subject up. It was surreal to feel like I had to walk on eggshells.

Every time I looked into those eyes, it was a throwback in time, to her precious little face, and the sister that I was protective about. I always heard old people say, that "They view their family and love ones through the eyes of when they were younger."

I always loved hearing the stories from old married couples, who had been married their entire adult lives. I wondered if I would ever find that person who I would grow old with. Similarly, I wondered if my sister would find someone that she would really grow old with.

We had both been through a divorce, and yet she couldn't even imagine what I was going through, because she was divorcing a normal man. I was married to and divorced a man who played with G. I. Joes on the floor of our den at two in the morning. I could have ignored it, but the dolls were having conversations with my husband as the ventriloquist. I would have gladly traded places with my sister.

My daughter had been in my sole physical custody since she was a toddler, and I had put her through the best schools, and she did great in school, as an honor student for the most part. She was an outstanding little girl. I only had a challenge with her behavior, once or twice in her whole childhood. I mistakenly never gave her many boundaries, because I thought she didn't need them. I was one of the only parents I knew who could say that my daughter was never spanked, because I didn't believe in it. I prided myself on it.

I wanted my daughter to have a larger sense of family. My father and my sister both spent time with her, and I thought she had a solid sense of family. She seemed to be excelling in school and was very creative. Her father, Mark, she, and I, had all worked on my film teaser, and had a wonderful time. When I got in the way of the *Romeo and Juliet* story that involved an inappropriately older man, all hell broke loose. After they were discovered together by my companion Mark, I was given an ultimatum. "Mark leaves or I leave," my daughter said to me in the kitchen one day. I didn't think that ultimatums were the way to handle things. I had even heard Dr. Phil say, "Teenagers don't rule the roost," so I said "Let's talk about this." She went into her bedroom and slammed the door, and the next day I was given a restraining order, alleging that I was abusive.

An overly zealous field investigator could not cite any incidents and was challenged by the judge who reminded her that I'm in a wheelchair and could not stand independently, so any of those allegations would be ridiculous. Also noted were her perfect medical records, perfect dental records, good grades in school until she rebelled. Some red flag would have arisen from close contact with peers and teachers every day, if she was abused. When children are abused someone notices it. My daughter was not. My daughter was beautiful, and had as I had always promised, got 100% of what she needed, and 99% of what she wanted.

After hearing the facts of the case and looking at all evidence and lack thereof, a Domestic Violence Court Commissioner dismissed the case with prejudice. He didn't see anything that constituted domestic violence and marked the documents accordingly. What was most heartbreaking to me was that it came down to an ultimatum, and when I did not comply, the consequences were severe. I could only hope that moving forward, my daughter would apologize someday, and find peace and happiness. She would always have my love and my forgiveness.

CHAPTER THIRTY-TWO

The Circus Begins

I had family members in Florida, and I was thinking about looking into some medical possibilities at the Mayo clinic. My boyfriend and I made the move and found a little duplex for rent in Silver Springs. It was airy and spacious, and it seemed conducive to writing.

When my wheelchair rolled over the large ceramic tile squares, it made a loud clicking sound, that seemed to travel around the house in surround sound. The last time I had spoken with my sister was when I called her at her apartment in Canada, in December 2015, almost 2016. It seemed as though she was excited to hear from me. It was seldom that I could actually reach her because of our completely different schedules, and she was still traveling as an ambassador for *Suits*. I was really worried about our father because he could sometimes become reclusive, depending on his schedule.

I knew that if both she and I tried to reach him, I knew that whichever one of us contacted him first, would call the other. I said, "Meg, do me a favor, if you hear from Dad first, please call me and let me know. He could have a heart attack, and nobody would know it." With that she replied, "Yeah Babe, don't worry I'm sure he's fine, but I'll call him and I'll call you soon as I hear from him." I thought we had the bases covered, and it was always my contention that, that's what family does. We look out for each other. We talked a little bit about our lives, but I didn't want to make it about work because that always seemed so boring. She seemed really positive, and I wasn't sure if it was sincere or placation, but whatever it was, I didn't want to judge her and I just thought it was great to touch base. I was surprised when she said, "Babe, it was really great hearing from you! I'm so glad we could connect. Let's keep in touch."

As a grown-up woman, I believed that she meant it. I thought, since we are adults that, if she didn't mean it, she wouldn't waste her breath. I felt that for the first time, as more mature women, that we could finally establish a friendship based on adult challenges in our lives that we had in common. I thought we could certainly talk about our relationships, but we could also share the things we had, our passion for travel and food, art, shoes, and handbags. She loved shoes since she was a kid, and coincidently so did I.

We also shared a passion for entertainment. My film project was gaining traction, such as partial cast interest, and I hoped that one day we would share our successes. I was really proud of her for remaining steadfast in a very difficult career; that being acting. I knew because of her education, that she always had being a translator or something in foreign affairs to fall back on.

When she started making good money on *Suits* I was so tempted to say something about helping our Dad out, but I just hoped that she would volunteer it someday. Dad never brought it up, but that's the way he was; kind and chivalrous.

He never wanted any tuition money in return, but he was always a stickler for principle. I think it would've made him happy just that she cared enough to offer. When she called me to let me know Dad was OK, I was glad we had that safety net there, of both of us and maybe even my brother checking up on him. Meg thought it was silly of me to worry so much, but that was my nature.

I know that life can often throw curve balls, so I learned to never assume that people are OK. I thought it was always better to err on the side of caution and check in. Time passed quickly after her divorce from Trevor, and I moved to Silver Springs Florida with my companion Mark. I changed the venue of my film project and moved to Florida for budget and aesthetic reasons. Getting things moving in Florida wasn't as easy as I thought it would be, but knew we were close to making it happen. I started doing my homework and looking into the Florida film commission and other local resources. Within the first week there, we needed several things and of course we had to stock the refrigerator. When we got in the door from the grocery store, and Mark was in the kitchen unpacking bags, I was in the bedroom setting my purse down, and the phone rang. I answered it, and to my surprise, it was my dad. He was excited, but in a cautious voice he asked, "Are you sitting down?" I said, "Well yeah of course I'm sitting down, I'm in a wheelchair." My dad's favorite thing to say was always, "Cut to the chase." So I said, "OK Dad, cut to the chase. What's up?" I could hear the reluctance in his voice, and then he said contently, "Well I got a call from Meg. She's dating a Prince," he said.

I said, "Well OK so, what else did she say? Is he nice? I thought Trevor was Prince Charming. Who is this Prince?" I was thinking he might be from some obscure country, who is far removed, and has six names. My dad replied, "Well, he's British. It's Prince Harry." I said, "Dad, what exactly did she say?" "Not a whole lot, she just said, Daddy, I met a prince." What astounded me about that, was that she didn't say, "I met an amazing man." She said, "I met a Prince." It seemed that the title was the most important thing to her. I think when most people call their parents after meeting a new love interest, they open the conversation by saying, "I met the most incredible man or woman I've ever met in my life," and "He or she is perfect for me." "We have so much in common."

We were never a very sensationalistic family and having grown up in Southern California and in television, I never thought titles were impressive, because wealthy people and celebrities were everywhere, so I just thought, "Well if she is happy, great." Trevor was really amazing and very impressive and, of course, Grandma Markle loved him, so even someone like Prince Harry would have to rise to the level of Trevor, in order to seem impressive. That being said then, what was impressive to us, was a sense of family, respect, kindness, inclusion, and caring. We didn't know anything about Harry. So I was somewhat blasé in my response, until more was revealed about him.

My dad informed me that the news broke, and that very likely the media would be searching the pipelines looking for family members to talk to about the fact that Meg and Harry were dating. I thought that was kind of silly because, if they were only dating, that's not really a big deal, so why would we have to be on guard worrying about people asking us questions. My dad said, "Just avoid the media, and someone will be calling us to brief us on how to deal with it." I said "OK, that sounds reasonable, but when?". He had no idea, and I didn't really think anything of it. I thought most likely they would stop dating, and nobody would call us, so why worry about it. It crossed my mind though that this new love interest could end up being just as hurt as Trevor was. I said "Well, this could turn into something good and maybe she will grow old with him, and he could know that his youngest baby girl was in good hands." That's what Dad really wanted to know more than anything, because sheds been through a hard time, and I think we all felt that everybody deserves to be happy, maybe this could be it. Honestly, I would not have expected her to meet a Prince. I thought she would end up with an actor, or a musician in Los Angeles. I always thought there would be some big announcement that she was dating someone who was considered to be Hollywood royalty. But because of our geographical location, I don't think we would've expected she would meet someone who was part of British royalty.

Over the next couple of hours, my phone started ringing off the wall, but it wasn't the media calling me, it was friends and acquaintances, coming out of the woodwork, and calling to let me know that they read in the tabloids that my sister was dating Prince Harry. I thought "Wow, word travels fast!" It was odd to me that tabloid readers knew what was going on, before we did. It turned out that my dad knew for about six months but was keeping it a secret. I thought that made good sense, on the grounds that relationships don't always work, and you don't want to blab to everyone, and have them get excited and start planning weddings, unless you know it's going to last. What confused me, was that, if they'd been dating for six months, that suggested that she would've been dating Harry, at the same time she was dating the restauranteur, Corey, who seemed like a good fit, because they both loved food and had exquisite taste.

I imagined that Corey would be devastated by being dumped for a Prince, or was she dating them both simultaneously? I was sure it could be uncomfortable for either of them. I called my dad back, to see if he could get a feel for whether or not she was doing OK, with all of the attention, and pressure that was building, because they had kept their relationship a secret.

I wanted to at least make an effort. I said, "Dad, maybe I should call Meg." I still had her number in Canada, but I said Dad, "Let me have her number in case she's changed it, or I don't have the right one in my laptop. I said, "Maybe she needs some family support, because this could all be very weird for her." Dad said, "Yeah, that would probably be a good idea. She's a little freaked out by all of this but give it a try." I wanted to see if she was happy and do my best to let her know that she had a support system. Throughout my life when things were going wrong, I had reached out for advice or just a shoulder to cry on and assumed that she might need one also. Many people idealize finding that special someone. I found myself putting my own lens and ideals on her life, when really I had no idea what her priorities were, and maybe she just wanted to play the field rather than finding Mr. Right after her divorce. Later in the afternoon, I called Meg and her voicemail came on, so I said, "Hi Meg it's me Babe, just wanted to say, I heard the news, and it probably feels weird, and overwhelming, but if you need to talk, I'm here." I assumed she would call me whenever she could. Hours went by, and I thought well maybe I'll get lucky, and I'll just try and get her. Maybe she didn't get the message. I called and heard her say, "Hello," I said. "Meg, it's me." I heard some commotion in the background that sounded like Doria, and then the phone went dead. I called my dad and said, "What is going on? I just tried calling Meg. I know she would not hang up on me, but it seemed like she did, or Doria did." Dad said, "I don't know, what is wrong with them, I don't know what's going on." I said, "I already had her phone number, and I had spoken with her a year prior. She was very nice, so I don't know why she would hang up, or if she did, it is just the weirdest thing. It was very rude," I said. "Well, Dad if she calls you, just let her know I'm here, and I understand she's really busy, but that made no sense at all. I know she's overwhelmed, but I couldn't imagine what happened, unless people were bombarding her front door, and she had to hang up." She had never hung up on me. I heard something going on in the background, that sounded like a crashing, so I didn't know whether something was wrong or not. I thought, "She could've been hurt." Silly me.

CHAPTER THIRTY-THREE

The Queen Would Be Appalled

I had a whirlwind day, because sitting in wheelchair all day is tiring, and I felt like I had just climbed Mount Everest. Mark was putting some things in the dresser, and I was sitting near the bed in my wheelchair, as the phone rang. I expected the phone to be ringing off the wall, but I didn't feel like answering it, because I was so tired. We made the mistake of answering the phone. It immediately opened into speakerphone mode.

A soft-spoken British journalist was on the other end asking a few questions, and I agreed to speak, thinking it was just a casual conversation. He began asking questions about our family, and my sister's tenacity. I said, "Well of course she's 'driven' and worked hard to get to the top". He said, "Would you say that she is pushy?" I said, "I don't know about that, I guess as woman, we do push. We push through the 'glass ceiling,' we push our way to the top. Sure, I guess that's pushy, if that's what you want to call it." I remembered all of her boisterous moments in the past, and I knew she could be very pushy, but I didn't want to tell that to a journalist. I thought that by saying that, I was giving her a boost in terms of being a go-getter, and that maybe that's what the royal family wanted to hear, so I went along with it. He asked if I my sister was a social climber, which I replied, "Of course women have to climb to get to the top. Yes." I felt like I was playing a word game. Coincidentally, I had coached my boyfriend on mimicking British dialects, so when the gentleman on the phone asked what the Queen would think of my sister, from across the room, my buttinsky boyfriend, said in a dramatic British dialect, making him sound like Julia Childs, "The Queen would be appalled!" I could have just shriveled, because he embarrassed me like that. In retrospect, I realize that I was being asked a series of leading questions, and then my boyfriend threw that in. The whole conversation seemed to crash into a mountain. Within a day, the news went around the world, with a bold headline labeling my sister as "Princess Pushy," and a shocking headline that graced online publications and print publications, that said "The Queen would be appalled." First of all, my boyfriend said that, I didn't. I was about to learn the hard way that aggregate news has a way of twisting and changing or labeling things far out of the realm of what they were intended to be. Unfortunately, a bold font headline has lingering labeling effects. Newspapers in some of the smallest towns on the opposite ends of the earth were saying that I bashed, slammed, and called my sister Princess Pushy. At first I thought it was a joke, and it was meant to be funny, but the social aftermath was anything but funny. Those labels caused a negative cascade of social reactions.

It was my contention that, if someone saw my mouth move, they could believe what was said. I believe in telling the truth, even if it makes me unpopular and, that being said, I began trying to set the record straight. I've always been one to confidently accept responsibility for what I say and there was so much out there that were not my words. Nobody could possibly understand that I didn't say some of what was printed, and I did say that, but I didn't mean it that way. I had to laugh because I was finding myself tangled in something that I would never be able to clarify.

At the time, I was worried that my sister's feelings would be hurt, not understanding what was real, what I meant, and what was not real in the articles. It seemed like she was not worried about me or the rest of the family, as she had never acknowledged anyone in the Markle or Ragland family, except for her mother. The situation started to feel like a double edged sword, in that I loved her and didn't want to hurt her feelings, but I started realizing that she was not speaking publicly, or saying anything in defense of the family. I still did not hear back from her, and began to worry about her, because I thought she must be reading what was in the headlines, and not understanding what I really said and what I didn't say.

One thing became apparent, and that was that she could've called me or gotten a message through to Dad somehow. We even wondered if, because of Royal protocol, maybe she was not allowed to contact us for some reason. We had no idea what was going on, and the idea of her being prevented from contacting us somehow felt better than thinking that she did not want to contact us. By the time the first interview hit the media, she must've had some sense of the fact that our family was being preyed upon, because the world wanted to know more about our family. She knew that I'm in a wheelchair, and that our dad is getting up in years, so I was hoping she would be a little bit compassionate and tell us what was going on, and what we should or should not say. I felt she should've communicated. She didn't call me.

Although I didn't hear anything from her, I still wanted to protect her depending upon the issue, or rather, make her look good in the eyes of the British people, and the British family, by explaining what our family is like and showing them that we are intelligent and articulate. At the same time, I felt foolish realizing that no consideration was being reciprocated. I have a surgical device that allows me to be more flexible. It dispenses medicine into my spine. The pump had flipped inside of me, so a surgeon had to go in and flip it back. I was really under the weather, and still had bandages around my chest and abdomen. I was in no mood for interviews or being seen because I was having a hard time just sitting up.

Entertainment Tonight contacted me and asked me to speak to some of the articles that had come out, and to discuss our family. I didn't feel good, but I wanted to do it, so that my sister could understand how I felt, and at that time I was really hopeful that she would rise to the level of being comparable to a combination between Lady Diana, and Condoleezza Rice. I felt very conflicted because, although I wanted to defend her, and be supportive, her silence was an insult. I am a very honest person, to a flaw, and had always been told that I had foot in the mouth syndrome, because I spoke my mind, and sometimes without careful consideration. I found myself in between a rock and a hard place, because I was hoping she would live up to that image, but it was also feeling that she was behaving in ways that were not consistent with that of a humanitarian, especially avoiding reaching out to our family. Much of what we were seeing in the media, was put out there by PR staff, so we couldn't tell how she felt, and we didn't have the opportunity to tell her what we said or didn't say. Even early on, it felt like we were caught in the cycle of setting the record straight and then having to debunk social media rumors, and labels that were really not appropriate, but that were a product of aggregate news. The public started getting the perception that we were doing a multitude of interviews, because many publications say things like, "We spoke with Samantha, and she said blah blah blah." Readers didn't understand that if I did one live interview, hundreds of publications wrote stories, and used excerpts or footage, or still photographs out of that interview, creating the appearance of us being interview junkies. I could not get around that much in my wheelchair, if I wanted to, so at the same time, I was upset by it, I also had to laugh. It was bittersweet and although I could laugh, by now I knew that my sister was probably not laughing.

I felt so ridiculous in that interview because my hair was dry from medication, I was exhausted, and I could hardly move. I didn't have the energy to sit there, but I tried to be a trooper, and be supportive of my sister. What may have seemed a fun interview, was not. I literally thought I was doing my sister a favor, because the world and the royal family knew nothing about our family. While we were being gung ho. thinking we were doing a good thing, we had no idea that because of cultural norms, the British people didn't think it was appropriate to speak about family matters.

It was very hot outside, but I enjoyed the heat and the humidity of Florida. As I rolled out my front door one morning to go to the bank, my neighbors across the way opened their door, and I knew that they recognized me from a tabloid, or my interview. I had to ask them to please be discreet, and let them know that we are a very normal family, and I didn't want everyone in the neighborhood to know about my sister.

Although I never expected that we would have to think about the issue of race as a source of conflict when we were adults, I was horrified at seeing racial slurs not only in social media, but in mainstream media. Negative racial remarks were made about my sister, but it seemed as though the media, especially social media, was trying to create racial divide by saying the white side of the family, or the Black side of the family. As far as I thought society had come in removing labels, especially racial labels, I was appalled that the media was allowing a social focus on the skin color of family members. I felt like the social emphasis on skin color could have deleterious social consequences.

On several occasions on Twitter, I saw my sister referred to as a few horrible names, and I had to draw the line. I had to defend my sister, and I was repulsed by the racial slurs. It was as in most families, that I could remark or call her a name, but I was irritated if anyone else did. I was feeling that, if I was disappointed in my sister, and we had issues in the family, that was our business, and for the public to start slinging racial mud, was very hurtful and inappropriate. I also found myself defending Doria a couple times, and I was kicking myself for doing that, on the grounds that I knew she would not do the same for me. I defended my sister, but she never knew it, and I suppose that it didn't matter, but I was just surprised that the public would even discuss skin color, and moreover, in a derogatory manner. We were an interracial family, and in my lifetime, I was proud to be a part of so much progress since the civil rights act was implemented in 1964, and I wished that Dr. Martin Luther King Jr. could be alive to see interracial families as becoming the norm. I was born in a generation that started seeing great change, and I felt trapped in an historical event that could potentially re-ignite racial tension with my family in the thick of it. As a family, we never called ourselves the white members or the black members of the family, and thought the public was unjustly taking it upon themselves to address us that way. It seemed like we were being socially played against each other. I could only imagine what the Raglands were feeling.

Over the next several weeks, the tabloid presence of our

family, and stories about my sister and Harry were becoming more salient. I didn't see what the big deal was, because they were only dating. I was starting to become irritated with the media's need to know so much. I asked myself, "Who cares who we are, he's not marrying us." Apparently, a lot of people did care, and were emotionally aligning with my sister and Prince Harry, in their modern fairy tale romance. The world seemed like it was needing a real life fairy tale, especially one that for the first time in history, represented the real possibility of racial and socio-economic equality. There had always been so much social conflict between races and classes, that this union seemed to carry the possibility of alleviating strain at a minimal and bringing about equality as the ideal. I got a call one morning from a quiet soft spoken voice, but he sounded so young and innocent, that I automatically trusted him, which was my first mistake. He said he just wanted to come by the house and talk a little bit, and get an idea of our family from looking at our photo album, recalling some of our favorite stories about the family. I agreed, knowing that I would limit what I said to him anyway, and give him boring pictures, that really meant nothing and were vague. I knew not to give everything away.

Mark was jumping up and down, turning six shades of green, and argued that it was a stupid thing to do, to speak with him at all. I thought it would be interesting just to see what he had to say, so we tidied up the house, and put important things away so he could not see them, including photographs or anything else that was sentimental. The next morning we got up early, and got dressed and of course cleaned the house, we knew that our sneaky little journalist friend would probably show up early and hide in bushes to get pictures, or put a recording device somewhere outside the house or on a window. Most people would say I was paranoid, but we soon found evidence to support that I was justified in my assumptions.

From the living room, I could see through the window blinds, that a small black car had pulled into a parking space across the street from ours, at the time the journalist was supposed to show up. He wasn't just a journalist, he called himself an investigator on another website I found, so I knew he had something up his sleeve. He sat in his car for an extraordinary amount of time, which raised several red flags. I thought well, "Two can play this game."

We put several recorders in the living room, and a small video camera facing outward that he would never see. When he came to the door, I tried to remain expressionless, and hide my urge to laugh, because he was quite small in stature, and dressed like Elvis Costello. He had heavy black horn rimmed glasses on his head, and a pair of cool Doc Martens shoes on his feet. In my old music aficionado days, one of the music trends was English Ska music. This gentleman could very easily have passed for a Madness band member. Well, if I wasn't so skeptical, I would have immediately liked him just on the grounds that he was adorable. He looked very studious and nerdy. It was all seeming too good to be true, and I started to feel a little bit suspicious. He was carrying a large backpack with him, which was also a red flag. When he came in, I immediately insisted that he sit down and make himself comfortable. We talked for a while, and he was oddly anxious to look at my photos on my devices online. I wasn't really comfortable with that, so I pretended to stumble around trying to find a password for my account, and with his eye on my computer, I purposely did not go into my photos. He probably had a recording device in his backpack that could scan other devices and snag my photographs.

He suggested that he needed to go to his car for a few minutes, but that he would be back, to allow my companion and I to talk. Mark was really aggressive with journalists who came to the house, to the extent of being embarrassing, and I was always used to being professional, in any business or entertainment communication. I agreed to listen to what he had to say, but I was more irritated with my boyfriend, than I was with the journalist.

After this journalist stepped outside, both Mark and I looked in the living room, to see that there was the backpack, set centered in front of the couch. We looked at each other and nodded, as an indicator that there was probably a recording device in the backpack.

The gentleman came back in and he didn't realize that we were skewing everything we said, to throw him off, because we knew there was a recording device in his backpack. While he was gone, we whispered or pantomimed everything out of sight, so if it was a visual recorder, he could not see what we were saying. I was diplomatic, and eventually we ended the conversation with the journalist being disappointed, because he did not get what he wanted. I said, "Let's stay in touch". I had heard that before, so it was almost as familiar as the Hollywood phrase, "Let's do lunch." Famous last words, I learned.

CHAPTER THIRTY-FOUR

Sealing Off the Hatches

I was exhausted when the reporter left, and I had a bit of cabin fever, so we dashed out the door as if we had been locked inside of the house for a month. Clearly we had not, but I was feeling really claustrophobic about my phones ringing, and people coming to my house with the intent of snooping.

When we got back, Mark noticed that the bar lock on the back door, had been partially pried in an upwards diagonal position. We realized that whoever wanted my photo album, probably tried to break in when they saw us drive away, so I decided to enact a community watch system, wherein my neighbors were aware of what had happened, and would keep an eye out and if they heard or saw anything, they would call me. I had a security system, but that week it was not installed yet, because we had just moved in. Prying the back door open would normally dispatch police, and the alarm would be loud enough for the neighbors to hear, but it was not on.

Little did I know that one of the television entertainment shows had knocked on the doors of our neighbors and gave them their phone number, and said, "Let us know when she comes out of the house, and we will give you a bit of pay for the tip." So, I knew that my neighbors would be on the take in a conflict of interests position. I had asked for them to keep their eyes on the lookout, and so had the journalist. Whoever offered the biggest tip wins. Everybody had everybody else in check. The only problem was that I knew that the journalists could pay the bigger tip. I hated to have to move, but I didn't want a replay of someone trying to get in the back door again, so a friend of ours offered us a bigger house that he also owned, that we could rent indefinitely. Although I dreaded the idea of moving again, because it was so exhausting in a wheelchair, even if I had my boyfriend's help, I would gladly do it for a larger house, and I swore that I would never move again. The expense of moving was lofty, but I didn't feel secure, so I really had no choice. By now there had been hundreds of articles, and my sister knew what we were going through as a family.

We felt like we were doing articles not for pay, because only some offered a small bit of pay, but we were doing it to defend ourselves, because we saw that on such a grandiose scale, that people were writing articles even though we had never spoken with them. What was so shocking, was that the articles were often untrue, and were skewed for the sake of sensationalism.

I spoke to several attorneys who advised me that many of the attorneys for the publications have very deep pockets, and unless you are incredibly wealthy, you cannot afford to sue them, because they don't work on contingency. This translated into the unfortunate fact that you have to pay those attorneys upfront, and every time they make a phone call, they charge an absurd amount of money, just for small tasks. By the time a week passes, your retainer is almost gone, and you haven't even begun to file the lawsuit. Publications know that everyone cannot sue them, which is part of the reason many they take it upon themselves to write whatever they want to.

I never understood what President Trump meant by fake news, but I certainly understood it more with every passing day. Another television show wanted to do a quick little interview, just like the previous one had, to get a sense of what our family was about. I met some lovely people on the interview team and the crew. By this time, I had not heard from my sister, and the stories that were promoting her as an incredible humanitarian, were not consistent with what was going on in terms of the family being ignored.

I really cared about my sister, but I felt like I had to be honest, so that if she was watching, she would understand what was going on with her family, and that we were somewhat cornered by the media trying to make her look good, and yet we were starting to hear that we weren't supposed to be speaking out, as we were trying to set the record straight and put fires out. Well, when the media was disparaging us, we had no choice but to speak out, and then it became a persistent cycle of setting the record straight. Even though I was being diplomatic, the media did not want to hear the truth simple truth, that family relationships are not unidimensional. They are complex, and even though I loved my sister, I was speaking out about behaviors that I did not like, and that were not consistent with the humanitarian fantasy that was surrounding her. People wanted to believe a fairy tale, but the reality was that there was no fairy tale, and the truth was being brushed under the rug, very early in the storm as the social tidal wave was rising. In my second interview, I was very forthcoming about the fact that I loved my sister, but she was not behaving like a humanitarian, and I was not seeing her as comparable to Diana. I didn't believe that Diana would ignore a sister in a wheelchair, and the entire family, especially since there was no logical reason for it. I was horrified to see suggestions in chat rooms that I was a jealous old hag wanting handouts, rather than having empathy for the fact that I am in a wheelchair. I felt like I was back in the 1600's in Salem Massachusetts, watching people throw stones at me, before they burned me at a stake. After that interview, there was a handsome British photographer, who took some pictures, and I was telling him the story about the unscrupulous journalist reporter, who had been at the house, and I was discussing some of the unsavory tactics of paparazzi, because I had dated a paparazzi photographer in Los Angeles. I knew the game. I was mortified when he so diplomatically smiled, and said, "It's not them you have to worry about, it's me you have to worry about." He left, but I knew that there was truth in his jest. After that I knew that, at any moment, a photographer could be hiding far down the street in the bushes, taking pictures of us. I made a regular habit of peeking in the direction of bushes, as a result of that interaction. I had worked as a part-time private investigator for a few months at one point in my life, and because I had photographed Workmen's Compensation claimants, who were engaging in strenuous physical activity, fraudulently, under the category of necessity of life activity, when they were supposed to be seriously injured, I knew how accurate those cameras could be. It was very sweet that he informed us of that, and I was not upset with him. I just wrote it off as the nature of the beast in the media business, and that it would be normal, moving forward. Life for many American families seems to center around holidays. On Thanksgiving day, we were really busy, but it was bittersweet, in that we were happy about the holidays, and had a lot to be grateful for, but a bit sad because we could not all be together. I was happy to find out that my father had spent Thanksgiving with Meg and Doria. Harry was quite gentlemanly to rent a house in Beverly Hills for the event, even though he ended up not going. Because it was a location that would be convenient for both Dad and Doria, he had to travel from Mexico and she was in the Baldwin Hills area of Los Angeles. The house was complete with a chef, butler, serving staff, and of course security, and enough privacy that it would be like a holiday at home, except for the fact that a chef cooked the turkey.

I was hoping that my father was able to have a proper meeting with Harry, but it was top-secret whether or not he actually showed up. Sources said that he was on a tour of the Caribbean at the time. I thought maybe Harry was really there, and my dad was just sworn to secrecy. A couple of articles came out saying that she was spending Thanksgiving with her mom, but Dad was also there. I was really glad that my father was able to have that, before being what I could describe as, nothing other than pushed out of the picture, or ghosted.

I was thinking about the fact that my brother and I were not included in Thanksgiving festivities, as a sign of things to come. It was as though someone had sealed off the hatches, intentionally. It was she who said when we lived in Woodland Hills, that the name of her business was "The Three Cherubs," rather than five. I didn't understand why there seemed to be a rush to seal off the hatches. It all made sense.

I wondered if she was worried that something would leak out, or if she was trying to keep family from getting in. I started to feel like our life was part of a circus, in that what people could see from the outside was completely different than what was going on behind closed doors. We had no idea what was going on, but it was becoming more obvious that she had more power to communicate with us and she did not. She didn't behave so oddly when she married Trevor.

CHAPTER THIRTY-FIVE

The Markle Circus Performers

The Circus was on the move, and we put the Big Top up, in Ocala Florida. Our new house was twice as big as the duplex we were just renting. Even though it was on a corner in a quiet area near horse farms, and local rural businesses, we felt like we had some privacy. Our house was a comfortable ranch style home, and we loved the backyard, because it was quite large. I assumed that I would be spending a lot of time out there getting sunshine, writing, and getting my ghostly white legs tanned. It was a great idea until I learned about fire ants. Within seconds of standing in the grass, one's legs would be covered with stinging biting fire ants.

I had enough of the media news about my sister dating Harry, and I was worried about Trevor. The way she rudely mailed his rings back to him, rather than being a compassionate adult and speaking with him in person, was very representative of her regard for people in general, in my opinion. I fluctuated in my feelings of protectiveness, as it became evident that she was avoiding doing the right thing by family and by others.

On November 27, of 2017, news broke around the world, that Meg and Harry were engaged. I had a knee-jerk reaction to call Dad because I knew he would have mixed feelings. I wanted him to be happy, and I was hoping that somehow he could be part of a fairy tale wherein his little Meg, grew up, married a prince, lived in a castle, and everyone would live happily ever after. The banter and fanaticism began chaotically stirring on the Internet, and even within our family, there was a nervousness, that was like something out of the *Twilight Zone*. The media began provoking family members, and pitting us against each other, by creating false stories, and forcing us to react quickly, back-and-forth, like a psychotic racquetball game. Everyone in the family was at each other's throats, but what was most interesting, was that rather than calling each other to find out what was said and what was not said, mudslinging was the reflex, rather than open communication and extending the benefit of the doubt. I was publicly flogged for honestly speaking my mind, and no one in the family had the nerve yet, to step out of the ant line. Every fairy tale had to have a villain, and I guess they picked me to be just that. Some of us in the family were speaking to each other, and others were still sucking up to media, giving interviewers what they wanted to hear which involved disparaging me. I wondered when the time would come that others would have the nerve to speak the truth, but for the time being, that wasn't happening.

The one thing everyone wanted to know in the public, and within the family, was who got an invitation, if anyone did. We waited, and as the days passed by, reality settled in like an atomic blast, when none of us got one, and it was obvious that none of us would get an invitation. Out of respect and traditional inclusion of family, Meg could have mailed invitations, whether the family could attend or not. I wouldn't complain but it was reported that more than 300 invitations would go out to complete strangers in the public. It was glaring that the issue was not a matter of inviting people based on how close they were or were not, because strangers were not close at all.

Because of that, it was even more hurtful, that neither the Raglands or the Markles were invited to the wedding. This was an incredible insult to our family, who had peers, and colleagues, and friends in our communities, criticizing us for not receiving an invitation. Uncles, cousins, everyone in the family, and even people on the fringe of the family, who had no business expecting invitations, were questioning why they not been invited.

The most insulting part of it all was, that in the eyes of the world, people were scrutinizing and seemingly shaming us, as though we had to be flawed for not receiving invitations. The absence of the invitation was as socially stigmatizing as a Scarlet Letter.

My mother whom my father divorced in 1972, and who had been married twice after the divorce, and had different last names, and who had never met Doria, and who only saw my sister in passing once at my graduation, really had no business speaking in the media as if she knew anything about our family. She and I never got along, and she was horribly bitter that I favored my father. She had only been to my house once, and she never came to our house in California. My brother's ex-wife, whom he was only very briefly married to, and divorced in the early 80's, never went to a Markle family function, would not allow our last name on her sons' birth certificates, had no business expecting an invitation, or discussing our family matters, because she was so far on the fringe of the family, and did not even use our family name. These people literally only interacted with my sister when she was under the age of 12, and only a couple of times when my nephews were toddlers, and my sister babysat them a couple of times. All them were sinking their teeth into interviews, and slinging mud at me to somehow make themselves appear closer to my sister, and to vilify me, because I expressed my opinion that my sister was not a humanitarian, and not like Princess Diana. Amidst all of the circus activity, my biggest concern was for my father, who had given my sister everything, always, and was a single parent to her for most of her life. I envisioned my sister rolling out the red carpet for him, and flying him out on a private plane, showering him with the accolades that he deserved, for everything. I could never imagine a more consummate father on the planet, and I had never met a father who was more praiseworthy, than our father was, and is as I write this. I was so excited for him, and yet I fluctuated between excitement, and being disappointed because he was being put off, and really left in limbo, wondering what was going on. I was in shock, when I realized that not only had she not called me on purpose, but she was playing games with our father. That seemed like the most cruel kind of games. I have never seen an instance where anyone claiming to be a humanitarian, could cruelly toy with the hopes and feelings of another human being about sentimental matters. I had heard that my sister's voice was kind and sweet, when Harry was in the room or nearby, but when he was not, she was cold and coercive. I started to realize that somewhere along the line, she had changed, and she was not the same person she was before, especially to Dad. I found myself constantly having to separate the sister that I loved with all my heart, and the sister that I loathed with all my heart. It would have been much more comfortable to be on an ancient torture stretch rack. The dichotomy was painful, and I felt guilt ridden for harboring any animosity towards her, even though I thought it was justified. I was always somewhat of a pushover and made excuses for others to adjust for cognitive dissonance that occurred when I was shocked by unkind or out of character behavior. It was a lot easier and less hurtful to think, "She's not ignoring us, she's just busy." I was really uncomfortable with the fact that it seemed like the media wanted to exploit our reactions or emotional pain and blast it on the world stage. It felt abusive and annoying, that anyone would want pictures of the family members who were allegedly not worthy of being invited to the wedding, as if we were circus sideshow freaks. Unbeknownst to us, there was an entrenched agenda going on in the media. I was already irritated by the sound of shutters going off in the trees, when we stepped outside of our front door, but I got used to it, to the point where I was ready to turn around, drop my pants and flash them my keister.

If I could walk, that would have happened. But I had to laugh all of that off. I searched my heart and soul and made every excuse in the book I could for her, and still I could find nothing even humane about the way my father was being treated by my sister. I didn't want anything from her, and with every passing day, I thought I wanted only that she would get rid of our last name, if she was going to be so cold hearted towards family. It didn't seem logical that she would disown the family and abscond with the name. I found it morally unconscionable, that the public would be so concerned with how she felt, and avoid looking at how an entire family was treated and felt. In December, we all hoped that there would be some word, or some extending of an olive branch, in light of the Christmas holiday, and the Christmas spirit bringing out the best in everyone. That's the way we hoped it would be. I watched again as my dad struggled through the cognitive dissonance of knowing that he gave everything, and loved my sister so much, but that she was able to turn her entire lifetime off with a switch. The media flooded cyberspace, television, and magazines with holiday decorations donning the streets of England, America, and church bells ringing everywhere, any reasonable person would be compelled to think that the holidays would prompt humility, regret, compassion and certainly gratitude. As tradition would have it, the spirit of Christmas is one of compassion and unity. On one day of the year, blessings are celebrated, and all disagreements and conflicts rest their weary heads under blankets of snow, and wake up refreshed after a feast and slumber, to embrace a new year. Sadly, that wasn't the case for our family. The ultimate insult to the family was levied, when in an open interview, Prince Harry said of his family, that the British royal family, were the family that Meghan never had.

I assumed that the British royal family were capable of doing a lengthy investigation, and that surely they would know that Meg had a significantly large family who loved her, and who were always there for her, and that our father gave her everything, always and in excess. There was a lot of love there, and in the tradition of Christmas love and unity, it was unconscionable, that she would not only ignore the whole family, but that she had somehow, seemingly brainwashed Harry into believing that she did not have a family, or that we were not there for her.

I doubted that Harry knew that when he was out of the room, her tone of voice was very different on the phone with my father, and that there was a duplicity lurking in the shadows, that he was unaware of. I got on my Twitter account after hearing him say that, and I said, "On the contrary, she already has a large family complete with aunts, uncles, cousins, nieces, nephews and marrying merely extends that family." Those were my words exactly, and I was bewildered when I read headlines the following day, that said, I bashed Harry. There was nothing in my statement that was bashing in nature, and I realized at that point, that there was likely an entrenched media agenda, to protect my sister, because she was marrying into the royal family.

What was so ironic was that I knew that the British Royal Family would be next, and I had said on Twitter, that "if she will treat our family this way, she'll treat your family this way." No one wanted to believe me, and so I was vilified around the world, and called every name in the dictionary on social media, and disparaging articles came out labeling me all sorts of horrible things. I had to come to terms with all of it. In my heart, I knew that I could live with the world flogging me because they did not know the truth, but I couldn't live with myself, if I did not speak the truth. Quite simply, I made it a guiding mantra that, "I would rather be hated for telling the truth, than be popular for enabling lies."

For the life of me, I could not understand how Harry could not have compassion for my father, on the grounds that there were enough photos salient in the media to show a lifetime of extreme nurturing by him, family experiences, and her education was more than 1 million dollars. Most reasonable people would understand that my sister was ignoring an incredible father, and her entire family in favor of being Royal. Many people around the world were mentioning the fact that she had bragged about our father in her lifestyle blog, The Tig. I noticed in several strategic articles a video a clip of a teenage Meg driving around town bragging to her friends that, "My dad lives up there, but we're not exactly getting on right now," to suggest to the world that there were grounds for ignoring him. The world did not know that the video clip took place when she was a moody teenager, and every teenager has moments when they don't get along with his or her parents. The reality of that video and the reason they weren't allegedly getting along was that she demanded that my father walk out on the production of *Damn Yankees*.

Dad was at Meg's wedding to Trevor, and was the one taking all of the pictures, so all these great things happened after that teenage video. In other words, the media blew that teenage video far out of proportion, trying to generalize it to their whole relationship to somehow justify her actions. This was seemingly a regular occurrence. I read an article in which my sister praised our grandmother calling her, her Queen and citing events like making apple butter with her. Our grandmother only made apple butter in the 1970s, when my brother and I were kids, spending the summers with her in Pennsylvania, and my sister was nowhere near being born yet. By the time my sister spent time with our grandmother, she lived in Florida, and was in a nursing home, and not making apple butter.

In defense of my grandmother's memory, I felt my sister was exploiting her to impress the Queen and play the matriarchy card. If my sister knew our grandmother, and honored her memory, she would posit self-sacrifice and compassion. Our grandmother predicated her existence on those principles. Since my sister talked so much about our grandmother, I thought it was very hypocritical for her to behave in ways that were in complete opposition to our grandmother's values. My father wasn't doing well, and although I had started him on a healthy diet, I knew that he was feeling fatigued and stressed out by the news of the wedding, and the public pressure on him to disclose whether or not he received an invitation. I spoke to him every day, usually a couple of times a day, to make sure that he was OK, and to see how his day went, and to let him know how mine was. I was morbidly surprised when I called my dad, and his voice sounded very hurt and dismissed. I said, "Dad, what's going on, what's wrong?" He said," This is really weird, she's not the same. When Harry is in the room, she is very sweet and a different person, but when he steps out of the room, she is mean and controlling." I said, "What do you mean by that?" I had a sick feeling in my stomach because I could sense what he was feeling. I had heard of crackle in his voice as if he were about to cry. For a man to be pushed to the breaking point of shedding tears only happened in response to death or extreme betrayal.

After a few minutes of silence, I said "Well, did you get an invitation? Did she tell you what's going on with the wedding yet?" He said, "I asked her, and she just said, lay low." I said, "You're the father of the bride, and you're supposed to be walking her down the aisle. What does lay low mean?" I could tell he was being given the runaround. I knew something was going on, but I couldn't put my finger on it. She had not come out in public, and announced how proud she was of Dad, and how she couldn't wait for him to be at the wedding.

My sister could've made a private trip to see him, or had a jet take him to England, to discuss the wedding, and share the excitement about it. It would've been as easy as a snap of her finger to do the right thing, and make that come to fruition. He was not some stranger, or distant relative. It was only right that she would want to put him on a pedestal, and shower him with love and gratitude on her wedding day. This was not as simple as a little wedding in Ohio, and because the eyes of the world were watching to see whether or not he got an invitation, it was really insulting that he had not. It was so uncomfortable for me to feel love when I looked at my sister's face, and at the same time, I realized that what she was doing to our father, wearing him down more every day, breaking his heart, and allowing him to be publicly taunted to elevate her own image, was heinous. The media were doing everything they could to make it look as though that was justifiable. But the world didn't know what was really going on, and how sinister it was. The world couldn't see that behind the smile and the wave, a very coldhearted and controlling woman who, rather than include, adorn and praise our father, was manipulative of him. I watched as the world insulted him on social media, for seeming as though he could not articulate a point, or that he was somehow inappropriate, even when expressing his desire for communication and his love for her.

The world had no idea what kind of pressure he was under, and how emotionally painful it was to walk in his shoes. I did because I heard it, and felt it, nearly every day. I was really horrified to see anybody on social media suggest that my father should shut up. During the same week, even though I didn't look in tabloid chat rooms, I got curious and noticed that there was an individual being particularly vile, and challenging me in a very personal way. Somehow this individual got my email address, and although I didn't want to wallow in the gutter with trolls, this email had a very personal and direct tone to it. The individual addressed me as Babe which was not yet knowledge in the media.

I was curious and willing to be open, to see what this person had to say and why he or she was feeling so inappropriately malicious. The emailed opened with, "In his heart-of hearts, Babe, Dad only has one daughter, and it's not you." I knew this was an incredibly competitive and jealous voice, lashing out in the email. This person was malicious and wanted to stretch out and somehow gouge me a bit. This person clearly wanted to be the center of attention, and because of the way it was phrased, I couldn't help but wonder if my sister was on the keyboard.

I was the first born to my father and was in no mood to play childish competitive games with a stranger, but I thought that most likely, I was not sparring with a stranger. "In his heart of hearts", was a phrase that my sister had used in The Tig. "Two can play at this game," I thought.

The Tango would be really boring as a solo dance. So I rolled up my sleeves, and replied, "It must make you writhe in your own envious swill, to know that all of your money, and all of your manipulation did not win Dad, all to yourself. And for the record I did get that ring, Meg."

When the game was all over, I was really sad to face the fact that, it was very likely that, her entire life, she wanted my brother and I, out of the way so that she could have all of the toys to herself. She wanted the family to be The Three Cherubs.

CHAPTER THIRTY-SIX

Princess Pushy's Ultimatum

I just shampooed my hair, and I was feeling a bit tired and dizzy, because I had a touch of the Flu. I was also feeling a bit sad about the holidays because our family were on opposite ends of the planet and being played against one another in the media. I think we were the only family I had ever seen, who could sing Christmas carols, while we were slinging mud. It would become apparent that if you can't beat the media, you join them.

Christmas was becoming somewhat of a tragic comedy. I called my father to see if he got his Christmas packages, and of course I asked him if he got a Christmas card or anything from my sister, and he had not. I said, "Dad, what did you mean by the fact that she was not nice on the phone, but when Harry was in the room she was nicer?"

He said, "It's more than that." With a cold yet sorrowful pause, he continued reluctantly, "She said "Dad, you don't need Babe and Tom. You don't need them!", to which he replied, "You're asking me to disown my kids? I can't do that! I love you all equally. I'm not disowning my kids. That's crazy. I am not gonna do that. You can't ask me to do that!". And then in a dismissive tone, she said abruptly, "Then I have nothing more to say. We have nothing more to talk about." In some distorted state of euphoria, she insisted to him, that she was an only child. He replied, "No you weren't". After hearing that, I knew what had probably happened. The only way to keep everyone from finding out the truth, was to keep everyone away from the wedding. People might start talking at the reception. I got the feeling that she must've told Harry a stockpile of lies, in order to garner some false sense of admiration. We really wondered what was going on with her, and then it became clear what was going on.

Dad went on to tell me what all of the game playing, and all of the suffering was about. In a deep coercive tone of voice, she said, "Why can't you just comply?!" I couldn't believe what I was hearing, as Dad went on, because I had just spoken with her in Canada about a year and a half prior, and she seemed like a completely different person. I felt like I was dealing with two different people.

The mere idea of her disowning my brother and I was ridiculous, as we were born first to our father, we had done nothing wrong, and we were her brother and sister her whole life. Although in our minds, we were a normal modern family, it was very likely that she had a different script running in her mind, and she wanted to be an only child. The more I thought about it, even though we tried to make her feel important, it was never reciprocal. I think at one point, she wanted the only child fantasy to be a reality, so when it came to the royal wedding, perhaps she thought she had some leverage to use to give my father an ultimatum, and she did.

For her to force our father to disown his daughter, who has struggled with MS for most of her adult life, and uses an electric wheelchair, and also his son, was so unimaginably cruel. I would roll out the red carpet for my family, and I am the kind of person who would call and see what they needed, and how they were doing and help in any way I could. I would've done anything for my sister, and when I worked on Matlock, I purposely made her the center of attention.

I started understanding that we really loved her, but that maybe it was one-sided all along. Because of our age differences, I was trying to be mature, and not look too far into things, but rather to let her be free to do her own thing. My perception of family dynamics were apparently much different than hers. I never made it a point to expect reciprocal effort from her. Maybe one of our problems as a family was that we never reinforced reciprocation and boundaries. I don't think my father ever expected anything back from Meg, so it wouldn't be unreasonable to think that we fostered narcissism. I could feel my father stopped in his tracks, as if he could not breathe, upon realizing that her demand or ultimatum was incredibly coldhearted, and nothing like that of a humanitarian. I didn't know if it was a genetic trait, or a generational characteristic, but I was astounded that a child could be so demanding of a parent, as to force compliance or suffer the consequences of some ultimatum. I experienced that with my daughter and couldn't believe that my father was also going through it. I guess the apple doesn't fall far from the tree.

Everything became as clear as the horizon.

It seemed very likely, that she thought that the royal wedding would be her bargaining chip to have our father all to herself, but only if he was willing to disown my brother and me. He could be included in the big ceremony and go to the royal wedding, if he would comply with her outrageously cruel demand.

Oddly, several publications referred to us as her estranged family members together and individually. If there was any estrangement, it was only because although we tried, and were involved in her life over the years, she apparently had better things to do, and had a different agenda. Meg hadn't spoken with our brother Tom either, and although he had some embarrassing moments in media, he praised her in the media, perhaps in hopes of getting an invitation. I was surprised when I read an article a couple of weeks before the wedding, wherein my brother warned Harry not to marry my sister. He said that marrying her would be the biggest mistake Harry could make in his life. In a bit of dismay, I recalled how many times publicly that my brother and other family members, and far fringe family members, insulted me for speaking my mind and the truth, and made rather disparaging remarks about me, suggesting that I was just jealous. I thought that they were all sucking up in hopes of getting an invitation, and that they would rather throw me to the wolves, than speak the truth and lose that opportunity. I found it quite ironic, that only after I had taken an extreme beating from the public in social media, and in mainstream media for my candor, that now others in the family, were coming out and saying what I had said in the beginning.

My brother embellished it a bit more, but he had also criticized me, not understanding how aggregate news works, for the perception that I was doing thousands of interviews, until he experienced it himself. I was really wishing that everyone in my family would have backed me and had the nerve to speak the truth from the beginning, rather than allowing me to do battle in the Colosseum by myself.

Amidst all of the media firestorms, what was most glaring to me, was the fact that I had seen several incidents wherein my sister and Harry had asked that the media be considerate, especially of my sister, and refrain from making racial slurs. I agreed with that and was sensitive of those issues going back to my childhood. It boggled my mind though, that at no time, did she and Harry step forward, and request the media be respectful of the entire Markle family. I watched as publications, and photographers, stooped to horrific lows by insulting my uncle who was not wealthy, but who was the bishop at his own church. He had retired from the Air Force, and sacrificed for his community and his congregation, his entire life. To see that he was being insulted, because his church was not the size of the church of England, angered me, and made me really feel that the world has become quite cruel. My sister watched as all of this took place and enabled it on continuum. I had a feeling that a lot of the articles that were negative about our family, that and said things like sources say, were really camouflage for her PR staff and strategies. It seemed reasonable, that if a whole family was being publicly disparaged, that out of decency she could have come forward and stop it, knowing very well that she had the power to, but did not, that she was effectively acquiescing to it. It all seemed to suit an agenda. The stress of the media, coupled with my sister's demand that Dad also had to keep the secret, while she smiled at the world, was too much to bear. I tried to distract him by communicating with him daily, making jokes and being positive but I knew that it must hurt him.

Valentine's Day rolled around, and I wondered what my sister and Harry would be doing for Valentine's Day. All I could think was that Harry would wake up on the floor one day next to the bed, realizing that there wasn't enough room in it for my sister, her ego, and for him. It would be an unusual situation of three's a crowd. Setting all jest aside, I still thought that my sister would have an epiphany, and apologize to Dad, after all, it is a day of love and giving. He did not get a call or a Valentine's Day card. Instead, she posted in an article about a piece on self-love that she had written in The Tig. I wondered when we would stop thinking that she would develop a heart, and do the right thing. I never forgot to wish my father well on Valentine's Day by sending a little special something, like cookies, or a Valentine's Day card by email, and then when I saw him in person, I could give him something. We made holidays work, one way or another.

What I loved about Dad and Grandma Markle was that it really was about that. Gifts were not important, and most of the time, a phone call, or a letter, was all anybody really wanted. I was happy just to spend time talking to him on Valentine's Day. I was elated, when I opened a beautiful red satin box from my father. It was a gold heart necklace inscribed with the words *Love Dad* on the front of it. In addition to that, there was a ring in the box that my grandmother was wearing when she passed away. The words "you're not getting that ring Babe," echoed in my mind like nails on a chalkboard. All I could think when I looked at the beautiful, gold heart necklace my father sent me, and Grandma Markle's ring, was, "Yes, I have Dad's heart, and yes, I got something better than that ring, I got Grandma's ring." Those two things are the most sentimental things to me, next to family photographs, and they are priceless.

That small voice in me always gave Meg the benefit of the doubt, and I thought that the little Meg that we loved so much, was still in there somewhere. I thought she just got buried with the overwhelming burden of fame and money. And I knew that money could be corrupting, but I didn't think it could corrupt so many in our family.

I had never given my brother my father's address, and phone number. Because I would not give up the information, my brother decided to show up at my uncle's house with a car full of journalists and baited my uncle into talking, and my uncle erroneously volunteered my father's location. In the days that followed, my father was bombarded with journalists at his house harassing him and forcing him to be reclusive after he learned that they would only take pictures and turn them into disparaging stories, making up whatever they could to insult him, and to shame him.

I got a call from someone offering to connect me with a photographer friend by the name of Jeff, who promised to discreetly take photographs of my father, putting him in an honest light, because other photographers had been so disparaging, intentionally. I received no money for the deal per my request, and the goal for my father was not money, because he had been turning down $50,000 interviews. It was just allowing the Royals and the world to see him in his proper light, because he was so horribly labeled and photographed. It was like watching vultures feast. The photographer said, "Don't worry, I will take good care of your dad, and nobody will even see." Just as one would put a positive photograph on a business card, I thought this made good sense. I agreed to it on the grounds that he remain 100 yards away and be discreet. I had been helping my dad on his diet, and lifestyle, and he was really doing great things like drinking vitamin water, and eating blueberries and chicken and fish, and getting in shape. He lived a beautiful lifestyle on the beach, so I thought it was important to portray him accurately.

What was mind-boggling, was that such a successful man, who had won Emmy Awards, and worked consummately in television for 40 years, could be treated with such disrespect, by people who only knew tidbits of misinformation that had been floating around in tabloid chatrooms and pubs. When I saw some of the photographs, I was delighted, until I saw an article that said he staged photographs. I nearly choked, when I saw photographs of the photographer walking 3 feet behind my father, as seen on an Internet Cafe surveillance camera.

I was guaranteed that he would not be visible, and I'm sure he knew that the camera was there on the ceiling, so I felt as though I had been baited, and so had my father. I was guaranteed it would be discreet, and then he publicly allowed himself to be seen walking 3 feet behind my father with the long lens camera, and furthermore, bragged about it on his Facebook page the following day.

I sent an email to the photographer, letting him know that I was horribly upset by what had occurred, and he said that he would arrange something with my father that would make him happy, and that he would fix the situation. The damage was done, and the thought of fixing it was tragicomedy at best.

I knew that everything my father had been through was far too stressful, and all he was trying to do was to reach out to my sister, express love, and allow the Royals to see a realistic portrayal of him. He had written a speech and wanted to go to the wedding but was repeatedly told to lay low. Whenever he asked about details, of when he would be going, or how, because he had not gotten an official invitation, I felt that he was being strung along, and I was progressively more perturbed, because I felt I knew what was going on, but I did not know how to tell him without crushing his heart. I knew that he was being played, because he would not comply with my sister's demand to disown my brother and I, as a condition of going to the wedding.

CHAPTER THIRTY-SEVEN

Truth Is Stranger Than Fiction

On May 9th of 2018, I spoke to my dad late in the day. I was worried about him, because he had been tired and saying that he was groggy but was having some strange pins and needles in his legs. I suggested getting on the treadmill, and massager, but really minimizing stress, and of course maybe seeing the doctor, to see if there was something he could do. I thought it was Sciatica. He was being bombarded by the press, and he had been photographed in an unfavorable light. Journalists stooped so low as to follow him to Home Depot, because he was doing a bathroom remodel, and purchased a toilet, and they had the audacity to print that it was his throne. What horrified me, was that I knew that my sister was watching all of this in the media, and she did nothing to protect him as his health was failing.

Journalists now knew where he was living. Some of them even rented houses up the street from him, so that they could have easy access to him, which forced him to be a lot more reclusive, and I knew that was really detrimental to his health. I was worried, because I had not heard from him for several hours through early evening, and I was speaking to him twice a day, prior to that. I called friends whom I knew spoke to him periodically, but who lived in another country, and no one could get a hold of him. I could feel my heart pounding, and I knew something was tragically wrong. I wanted to call the police in Mexico, or anybody just to have somebody track him down. I didn't hear from him until May 13, when he let me know that he was in a small charity hospital in Mexico after having a small heart attack, and all they could do there was stabilize him and his doctor had him go to Chula Vista Hospital in San Diego. He had a stent planted in his heart, and a filter to prevent clots from getting into it, but the stent procedure would allow him to be up and moving more quickly, and was a less invasive procedure than heart surgery many years ago, when open-heart surgery was performed.

I wanted to get out there, but at the time I had no way of getting out there and wheelchair accessibility would be a problem on short notice. I didn't know any of his neighbors. Additionally, the media would have bombarded us, while we were there.

I couldn't have any of that, with my dad recovering, as it would've been too much for him to handle. I felt very trapped, and I was quite angry with my sister for allowing my father to be there alone, with mediocre care. She could have made sure he had the best heart surgeon available. After all was said and done, I heard through the grape vine, that the royal family wanted to help my father and make sure that he was provided for, but that my sister rejected the idea. I was furious with her, but more than anything, I was brokenhearted by knowing that he could've been comfortable, and safe, but my sister said no.

I wondered what kind of monster would tell someone else that they could not help my father? There was no effort required on her part. I could not understand my sister's absolute disregard under such extreme circumstances. I felt as though she caused the extreme amount of stress that led to my father's heart attack.

Between the stress of the media, and having a sedentary lifestyle, the stress surrounding the wedding and being under emotional duress, I believe that his heart couldn't take it. I understood that the public couldn't understand why my attitude was the way it appeared. I knew everything that was going on, and I could not leak the information to the public. My father was being attacked from every angle, and in many ways, I felt powerless to protect him. After my brother sold out his location, putting him in danger, and my sister seemingly strong-armed him through the wedding by hinging his wedding attendance, on whether not he would disown my brother and I, coupled with being disparaged and prayed upon by the media, it was all just too much for him. I knew that, had my sister done the right thing by inviting him, and showered him with love, that none of it would've ever happened.

Tabloids went crazy suggesting that, because he was photographed carrying fried chicken, that he must not have had a heart attack. A few television personalities went so far as to opine that my father was clearly an alcoholic, because he was seen buying that Heineken for the guards who work for his gated community. I was appalled at the audacity, to be so rude and insulting, while knowing nothing about what was really going on. Just because someone is seen carrying Heineken beer, does not mean that he or she will drink it. Similarly, I had seen many pictures of that talk show hostess drinking wine at a table, so should I have inferred from that, that she was an alcoholic?

The point is that pictures are often skewed, and it's really unfair to make assumptions based on very limited visual and audible information. As a society we are so quick to label people we know nothing about, as easily as we inhale and exhale. The bigger the lie, the bigger the buzz, seemed to be the rule. Every fairy tale has to have a villain, or antagonist, and protagonist, and it seemed as though anyone who said anything that wasn't fluffy about my sister, was labeled as a villain.

The truth could create public dissent, and the fairy tale was moving along so well, that no one dare step out of line, speak the truth and risk public backlash. I was a bit sad, and yes, outspoken, because I always cared about the truth, and I thought it was the one thing that mattered in our evolving world.

Somewhere in our media experiences, I felt as though we were in the process of running into a clash of communication styles in that The British Royal Family are traditionally more reserved. Respectfully, I had heard that the norm for The Royals with regards to publicly sharing personal information, was never explain, and never complain. I was familiar with that philosophy, as it was a way of life for both of my grandmothers. I realized though that, it's easier to abide by that philosophy when people are extremely wealthy, and have a significant amount of control over politics and the media though public relations representatives. However, when commoners like us were on the menu as the entree being served by a steaming hot, entrenched media agenda, it seemed counterintuitive and even dangerous at times, to say nothing, rather than make an effort to set the record straight.

It was a Catch 22 situation, and as we all had bills to pay, and I am living with disability, I decided that when it was appropriate, and what I had to say seemed to have social utility, why should I not be compensated? The world was wanting to know about so many things, and I refused to lie helpless tied to train tracks bound and gagged. It was appalling to me, to think that anyone would assume that it was OK for media to make millions of dollars on us, while we struggled, and yet the interviewers took our time, and made exponentially more money than we ever could by using us as subjects. I believe in win-win situations, and I was adamant about the fact that, if they were going to make money, then so were we. I did not feel I had to apologize for that, because money allows us to survive. I knew that I could put some of that money towards adaptive equipment I needed in my home, so that I would be safer and be able to navigate my home. I had always been limited by living in apartments that were not mine to modify, and they did not have environmental modifications where I needed them to help me. I couldn't understand why or how people could be so cruel, as to not be willing to look at the fact that, if a woman with disabilities makes some money to be more secure and less limited by the environment as I was, then that should be a good thing. I certainly wasn't begging, or asking for charity.

I had worked in broadcasting, and in television, and was quite comfortable being outspoken. I saw nothing wrong with speaking publicly. Coincidently, becoming rich was not a goal, but becoming safe and comfortable with progressing disability was. I wanted the same security for my father.

On several occasions, I noticed that I was being insulted in the trenches of social media, because of my disability. In fact, I was even called a whiner. I had to ignore it, because I knew that I was dealing with media trolls who make it a hobby to prey upon people who are in the public eye. I wasn't going to let them destroy my self-esteem, and those grounds, I made it a point to be seen, and to speak out and not allow myself to be intimidated. I was not whining, but when interviewers asked me about my disability, I was quite open about it. No matter what I said, I found myself up to my ascot in social labels. I knew I had to continually put something else out on the scales for the public to weigh against media fabrication. I love gardening and being outside, but I was quite limited by being in a wheelchair. I could still enjoy the garden adaptively, even if it was only watering the flowers. As Mark handed me the hose, I heard a camera shutter sound, snapping off repeatedly, from what sounded like the tree near us. "Did you hear that.?" I asked. "Yeah, I hear it every day," he scoffed. Upon the realization, that we were probably being watched, I rolled around the front yard, and backyard in my wheelchair, looking for cameras in trees.

We got really tired of camera shutters going off in the trees, and seeing suburbans outside of the house following us and it almost was becoming routine and boring. I didn't even really mind it, because I always believed that in a public forum, people don't really have a right to privacy, so I was comfortable with it, but as with anything, there are boundaries.

CHAPTER THIRTY-EIGHT

Dodging Paparazzi

On May 16, 2018, I was called to a studio in Orlando to do an interview for Inside Edition. It was about an hour drive from our house in Ocala, Florida. We had to get on several freeways to go there and Florida has several areas that have tollbooths on the freeway. On the way back from the interview, we were near the intersection of I-4, and I-75, when someone with a camera in the vehicle, pulled up sideways so close to us that my boyfriend had to swerve the car, to avoid us being sideswiped. He was driving, and I was in my wheelchair, with the seatbelt going across my waist in my legs.

He pulled the steering wheel very hard to the right and swerved to avoid hitting a concrete barrier, which resulted in him then slamming on the brakes, which sent me flying over the seatbelt, and under the dashboard. I felt like a rag doll being thrown forward without the strength to brace myself. We could not stay in a parked position because traffic was moving, so Mark was panicking to figure out how we would get me off the floor. I was screaming in pain, so he frantically pulled into a tollbooth, to have a supervisor help him pick me up from the floor, and into my wheelchair.

When we asked her where the nearest hospital was, she gave us directions, and we went to Ocala Regional Health Center, where I was treated for bruises, lacerations, and a sprain of my ankle. I made the mistake of telling TMZ that I was injured in a car accident, and so from that, the world assumed that there was an automobile collision somewhere.

We never made contact with another vehicle, and we certainly never hit a concrete barrier, or someone on the highway. Cameras and highway officials would have seen it. Furthermore, if we had hit a concrete barrier, my vehicle would have been mangled. Only I was injured, and the only impact, was my body hitting the floorboards. Within a day, newspapers and tabloid articles around the world, said that, I staged a car accident. Because there was no accident, and no evidence of one, journalists decided to make one up.

My father was not outspoken at first, nor was my brother, but it seemed as though after I had taken extensive floggings in media and social media, because I was speaking the truth, then other family members developed the courage to step forward and speak honestly, rather than feeling as though they had to support a social fairy tale.

Understandably, there was a lot of social pressure on him to only be positive to some degree, because everyone was getting their hopes up that they could gain favor from my sister and Harry, or of other royal family members. The world, including the British Royal Family, would soon see that I was speaking only the truth. I knew that it wouldn't be long before the British Royal Family were treated as we all had been.

I had to separate myself from it, because I was dealing with serious disability, and my life was already very stressful. I knew the world could not understand what my life was really like. I could let it roll off of my back like water on oil, when I was being defamed, or canceled for speaking the truth, defending myself, and exercising my freedom of speech, but when I witnessed it happening to my father; before, during, and after his heart attack, I put a line in the sand, and became a staunch defender of him. Even though I struggled with disability, I felt as though I had more energy, than he did, to battle the Titans. I had had it up to my eyeballs, with aggregate news and defamation, libel and slander, that was so salient in the industry. Many sources knew they could not be sued because their lawyers had deep pockets, or billions of dollars, and they knew that little people like us could not go up against them successfully.

I was so glad when my father called me and let me know that

he was OK. It was such a terrifying thing to go through, in my opinion, and I couldn't understand how he could take being taunted by the world, after going through so much. Even though journalists were scrounging, trying to find him in the hospital, the media was all abuzz with news of his heart attack, and he was being mocked. Sadly, when he emerged from surgery that he very likely could've died from, there was no phone call, or balloons, or cards waiting for him from my sister and Harry. At a very minimal, I thought they would have the compassion to reach out to him, and be kind and apologize, and wish him a speedy recovery.

I had seen several suggestions the media, that Doria was going to walk Meg down the aisle instead of our father. I had also heard that Prince Charles was going to walk her down the aisle. I thought it was most noble of my father, that in spite of his heartbreaking disappointment, he was grateful that Prince Charles would walk Meg down the aisle, since he had had a heart attack. So many people asked me why my sister would want her mother to walk her down the aisle, and I knew that, that was not the plan from the beginning. The only reason that my father not going to be walking her down the aisle, was that he would not comply with her demand of disowning my brother and me. It was all a mystery to the world.

I was so sad for my father, and disappointed that neither Prince Charles, nor had anyone in The British Royal Family, made any attempt at contacting my father, to either wish him well, for the recovery or extend any kind words whatsoever. I felt pretty certain at that point, that my sister had probably said some very untrue things, that prompted the British royal family to treat our family with little regard. I couldn't understand why they would not take the initiative to find out for themselves, through proper meetings, rather than just accept whatever my sister had said. We read later in a publication that the British Royal Family suggested that my sister do the right thing, and take care of my father, but that my sister refused.

On its face, the wedding was a big beautiful grand event. When I removed the bells and whistles, it looked more like a beautiful red apple, that was rotten at the core.

At that point, I was convinced that unconditional love sometimes borders on insanity. I couldn't believe that because Harry had been outspoken about other issues, and he had spoken out publicly about the racial mudslinging, and he took her defense, that he would not also publicly defend my father, and speak out; advocating for our family being respected. My sister and Harry had met at Invictus, which is a worldwide sporting competition that advocates for veterans with disabilities. They had to know about my challenges, because they had experience with veterans who live with MS and other disabilities. I didn't want to be a crybaby, but it really seemed like a no-brainer that to totally ignore someone who is disabled, especially family, is not normative, it is in no way humanitarian, and is in no way compassionate. I kept thinking that maybe they're just really busy, because there's no logical reason that we should be ignored. I didn't even want sympathy, but it was the principle, that basic compassion, and consideration would've been appropriate, because it would speak volumes to everyone around the world who is dealing with physical challenge. And yet we would hold out for some fantasy idea that she would do a complete turnaround and have a heart.

I doubted that my sister would tell Harry or the Royals about her ultimatum. I didn't think that the media could be any more brutal than it has been, until I saw the headlines insisting that my father allegedly faked a heart attack, to avoid dealing with a photo scandal, and therefore not going to the wedding. Because the media could not contact my father in the hospital, they needed some drama, that would explain why the "Deadbeat Dad" as the media had called him, was not part of the fairy tale. I have never heard anywhere that a Deadbeat Dad could be an award-winning director of photography, who gave all three of us kids a great life in Southern California, including million dollars for his youngest daughter's education. A lot of kids around the world would love to have such a father.

My father was insulted for what he did not currently have in his life, which was wealth. It was astonishing to me that people couldn't understand that, if he's not wealthy now, perhaps it is because he has given everything to us, his family. He paid every penny of Meg's education, and provided great support for us over our lifetimes.

All things considered, a little bit of love, respect, and gratitude reciprocated, was not unreasonable. The media had to do everything in their power, likely at the behest of PR, to make him look bad, so that she would look better, or justified that she had not invited him to the wedding, as a cover up. The frightful truth was that it was likely a ploy all along, as a punishment for not complying with her demands.

I read a story about a gentleman who was making fun of my father because he was often photographed wearing hooded sweat jackets, because they were comfortable to him. Some jokester in social media, suggested that they just call my father Thomas Armani. That gave me a brilliant idea. I wanted to see if the media would just print anything they hear, without verifying fact. I knew they would, so I got on Twitter and posted about my father's upcoming hoodie line. The very next day newspapers everywhere, were saying that my father was coming out with his own hoodie line. I mocked it as predictable on Twitter, and one of the publications said, "Samantha got us again". That was my way of illustrating how unreliable and how true the term fake news really is. The worst was yet to come. I could understand that the world wanted a fairy tale to escape from social and political strain. The problem was that the real truth got buried, like the proverbial elephant in the room, in favor of a created truth to protect a social fairy tale. I struggled to maintain enough objectivity, to have faith that something good and beautiful, could be captive in the shadows, crouching behind something that was so wrought with deceit, yet so elegantly camouflaged.

CHAPTER THIRTY-NINE

Marrying The Markles

In spite of everything that was going on emotionally within the family, weddings are a new chapter certainly in the life of a couple, but also in the life of the family. In traditional weddings, the families of the bride and the groom become in-laws. I realized that even though we felt hurt and isolated, I was secretly optimistic that we could still experience a modicum of bitter sweet joy, thinking that maybe my sister would become happy, and more loving and mature, and apologize as a result, and that things would be different down the road.

Family events usually make people emotional, and it allows time to reflect on what is important in life. That being said, I was hoping that she would think about our family in the real sense, and maybe after the wedding, there would be some communication.

I felt like Jim Carrey's character, Lloyd Christmas in the film *Dumb and Dumber*, when he said, "One in a million? So you're saying, there's a chance!" I thought Princess Pushy would wake up one day, and realize that her demands to our father were cold hearted, and unrealistic, and maybe she would apologize. The probability of anything like that happening was one in a million. Wedding day was emotional for our family, and although I was trying to be happy for my sister in spite of everything she had done, I was feeling an extreme amount of sorrow for my father, because even through a heart attack, he would have to watch his little girl get married knowing everything he had been through, and that he had planned a speech for. He didn't get to share his beautiful hopes and dreams for the new couple.

To pour salt on the wound, sources said that Dad would not receive a coat of arms that is traditionally extended to the father of the bride when marrying into the Royal Family. I really believed that some part of the ceremony should have mentioned my father, and on the flip-side, I knew that it must be quite uncomfortable for the Royal Family to know that the wedding would be taking place without my father there, and that the circumstances that were involved were a mystery to them.

My father had a real heart attack, and I don't think anyone sitting in St. George's Chapel at Windsor Castle could imagine that it was seemingly all part of a cold game, designed to cover up the world's greatest snow job. Because the wedding was taking place in the church, I thought surely that my sister and Harry would be either moved by grace, or compelled by guilt, to do the right thing, at least in sentiment. Everything that was happening went against the grain of religious tenets. Well, it was not for me to say, but I was so confused by the fact that anyone would allow the wedding to take place this way.

The Royals couldn't postpone the wedding so that my father could be included, and I knew it was not unreasonable that they reschedule, given resources available to make that happen. I got up very early in the morning on wedding day, May 19th, 2018. I think it was 3 o'clock. I needed a lot of extra time to get ready because my companion had to help me to get dressed and prepared, and to get our house ready for the crew.

I had decided that I would watch the wedding with the world, and I was sharing it with a German television station. I assumed that the world wanted to know how I felt about the wedding. At that time, I don't think anybody really understood the internal dynamics of the family, and they certainly did not know the ultimatum that my sister had given to my father.

Although I wanted to see her happy, I was conflicted by the fact that I knew there was a duplicity involved that had put my father through a great deal of torment, and was historically unprecedented as a storyline, in a fairy tale that was situated behind a great deal of smoke and mirrors.

The headlines were flooded with every detail of the Royal

Wedding, except a critical truth. Some broadcasters and publications were talking about the fact that our family was not invited, and many were finding a way to justify that by discrediting us, and some were brushing it under the rug. Many of them tried to be professional, focusing on it as a world event, and what it symbolized for so many. Words like unity, and love were in the foreground of this wedding that cost upwards of $40 million dollars.

It was an emotional event for the British people, who had been supportive of and endeared to Harry, since the tragic death of his mother Diana. For many, the wedding symbolized the end of Harry's loneliness, and a happy ending for a biracial American Cinderella. The wedding also symbolized the perception of equality between race, and socioeconomic status, but that aspect of it was only mildly mentioned in the media. It was quite clear that this wedding was a triumph for so many people, who had aligned with my sister and Harry, to feel that finally the world had come to a place of love and color blindness, on the world stage. It meant something to so many around the world, whether they were little girls who always dressed up and wanted to be a princess, or the people who lived their lives thinking that there was such a separation of classes, and that equality would never be seen in their lifetimes. I was starting my morning, thinking about all of those things, and how great it was, even in a sordid way, to be a part of this historical change, and this symbol of unity. I say sordid, because even though we were naturally hurt by being excluded from the wedding, I was looking for the beauty in it. I was looking for the promise of change for the world, and the symbolism in it, so I had to remain objective in many ways. I wondered if Dr. Martin Luther King Jr. could have ever imagined a biracial royal wedding. I thought about it, and it meant a lot to me. I knew that so many people around the world were seeing the kind of change, that we had made to that point in evolution; where love should conquer all, and the wedding was against all odds in many ways.

I felt like we were finally at a place where his skin color didn't matter, and people looked at each other as people, allowing us to feel a common thread around the world, regardless of differences. Aside from the social equality fairy tale occurring though, my father was brokenhearted on top of having had a heart attack, my sister had issued an inhumane ultimatum, as a condition of going to the wedding. I knew that humanitarians don't behave that way. I doubted that my father was feeling warm and fuzzy, or philosophical about the wedding, and he was in the hospital.

I would hear from him later in the day, so I just prayed that he was resting, and would call me when he could. The talent and crew of RTL in Germany were setting up in my living room, and although my house was not huge, it sufficed and everything was progressing quite smoothly. I had dyed my hair dark, and although social media was making fun of me about it, suggesting that I wanted my hair dark hair to look like my sister, little did they know my hair was always dark, and blonde was a change that I made later. I darkened it, so that when I went to the grocery store, I wouldn't be recognizable from the earlier blonde tabloid photographs. Little did everyone realize, though, my natural hair color is dark. When it was time for guests to start arriving at the wedding, it felt so surreal, that so many people could be taking part in such a beautiful event, while knowing that the father of the bride was left out, and publicly mocked, after a heart attack.

The guest list was bursting at the seams with celebrity faces who really didn't know my sister, but who had been invited to make it as grandiose an event as the world would expect. The Royals were lovely in their appropriate formal attire, and I really enjoyed watching the variety of women's hats on display. With regard to fashion and aesthetics, I enjoyed watching the whole wedding. I had to focus on the fashionable aspect of it, to avoid the emotional aspect of it. When it came time for the attendees to go inside the church, I was elated that, not only was it a biracial and multicultural event, but the church was so extraordinarily beautiful, and I was in a distorted state of euphoria. The section of the church, and its pews that were normally reserved for the family of the bride, were empty, except for the pew occupied by one family member. Meghan's mother Doria was sitting there in the front row completely alone, and I couldn't help but think that she looked like a hockey player in the penalty box, wearing Oscar De La Renta. She looked dreadfully uncomfortable, but the discomfort seemed to be mixed with a wide variety of emotion, as might be expected from a secret toting mother of a bride who is marrying into the British Royal Family.

I also noticed that she was crying, and I wondered if she was crying because she thought she got away with something, or if she was crying because she was overjoyed that Meg was marrying her alleged true love, and he happened to be a Prince. The choir for the wedding was chosen by Doria, as was the Reverend, and never in the history of a Royal Wedding, had the choir and the Bishop been Black. Bishop Michael Curry delivered a sermon that moved not only audiences around the world, but I thought it had the power to move mountains.

I wondered if his speech would be the same if he knew that the entire wedding involved an ultimatum. Because he spoke so much of unity and forgiveness, I thought maybe he was tapped into something divine. It was the most beautiful sermon I had ever heard in my lifetime, and I was hoping that it meant something to my sister. I was hoping that she would think about it, and be unable to avoid being loving, and embracing to our father, especially after the entire sermon was recited with the force of a holy billboard.

At that moment, I said several prayers. I hoped in my heart, that Meg would think about her ultimatum, and feel so moved to make amends for it, that she wouldn't be able to contain emotions throughout the service. The power of love consumed the cathedral, and most of the world, as it spoke to voices of racial divide who had been silent for so many centuries. It spoke loudly to families about forgiveness. It spoke to us all, as human beings, about the truth that all things can be accomplished, if we work with the power of love, and that it is divinely within all of us. I wished that my mother's mother, Dorothy Loveless, was alive to see it. What I took from his sermon, left me more philosophical and emotional for the rest of the day, than the wedding itself did. I knew that my father was watching it, and I was hoping that he would find some peace in such a beautiful sermon. I hoped that there might be the possibility of my sister having an epiphany and being moved to act out of love and truth and contact our Dad.

I thought it was beautiful, and I was astounded at how gracious the British Royal Family were, to be so multi-culturally inclusive. The wedding was expensive, and it made such a loud historical statement, in such a grandly beautiful way. I couldn't avoid wondering how Doria could be so cold, as to sit there knowing that my father had had a heart attack, and that the wedding should've been postponed to include him, but I thought, "How selfish of her to sit there, and siphon all of the glory and beauty away from my father, and hoard it all for herself."

It really did signal back to the days in Woodland Hills, and all of the signs were there then, but nobody had a crystal ball. The wedding gift that I could never give my sister and Harry, remained boxed on the shelf up in my closet, in the darkness. I searched the world for the one gift, that I knew no one else would give them. I am not wealthy, so I wondered if it would be flashy enough. It's tough buying a gift for someone who has everything. Even if someone by chance had stumbled upon the same gift when shopping for her, I knew at least, that it could not duplicate the same sentiments. I wanted to give my sister something sentimental, and rare. I purchased it long before knew about the ultimatum. I was hoping that it would pull at her heart strings, and it would take her back to a more innocent place in time, when love, simplicity, and wonder, guided her days.

While the camera crew was waiting for me in the living room, I opened the closet door, pulled the box down from the shelf, opened it carefully, and stared sadly at the Reuge music box, nestled in white confetti. Although I purchased it for her from someone in Europe, it was the same as one that had sat on my dresser, and that she was so mesmerized by when she was little.

I stared at it for a moment, as tears rolled down my cheek, I understood that people sometimes change in ways that we cannot foresee, or moderate. I had a heavy feeling in my heart as I realized that I had to let her go, but I could not let go of the ultimatum. I could forgive her and not begrudge her, but I could not watch her continue waving and smiling, and burying the truth, as our family; especially my father, who was still being discredited and disparaged. I think it's reasonable to say that sometimes tough love has to come in to play. I always believed that if you really love or care about someone, it is wrong to enable lies, especially where they hurt others. I equate truth with love, and kindness, even though it might not feel good at the moment to those who avoid it.

All things considered, I had a grinding feeling in my stomach, because I had to sit and watch a fairy tale play out, that I knew was more like a modern remake of *A Tale of Two Cities* meets Pandora's Box. As I gazed into the music box, it took on a completely different meaning. The shadowy figure on the back wall inside of the glass dome, was reminiscent of my father standing there, locked out of my sister's world, but locked inside of a media menagerie.

I knew I was running out of time, and I couldn't share the sad secret of the gift with my guests, so I carefully put the box back up on the shelf, and closed the door, where the gift would remain in the darkness. When the wedding started, the camera was rolling for the German television station, and although I wanted to be supportive and positive, I struggled to hide my real emotions. I knew that I had to be reserved about some of my comments, because I knew that the world could not see behind the smoke screen. My sister's dress was beautiful, but the world had already begun to challenge the fact that her taste in clothing was overly expensive, and when juxtaposed with poverty around the world, it was a bit of an eyesore. Like the old saying, "It's not the dress that makes the woman, but rather it's the woman that makes the dress." The fact that PR had promoted her as the poster child for humanitarianism, drew attention to everything she wore and purchased. My sister's dress designed by Givenchy, reportedly cost $750,000, and of course the world was up in arms, as photographers were snapping their cameras, as loudly and energetically, as Irish dance sensations River Dance electrify stages, with the thunderous rhythm of their clogs. What was louder than the buzz of the wedding itself was the sound of social dismay, over the fact that Kate Middleton's wedding gown, designed by Sarah Burton, looked like $1 million, but only cost $299, which was minuscule compared to the cost of my sister's wedding dress.

As a media event, the wedding was breathtaking, but there seemed to be something missing. Not only was my father not in the cathedral, and the rest of us in the family would have liked to be there, but the most important thing that seemed to be missing, was the excited, childish, overjoyed anticipation that is often present when a bride and groom look at each other at the altar. Conversely, when my sister and Harry looked at each other, it seemed like an oddly, lackluster moment. So many rumors were circulating in social media that the entire wedding seemed staged. I was trying not to judge harshly, because the crowd watching the wedding was rather large, and certainly that could have contributed to nervousness of both bride and groom. I kept looking at my sister's eyes, and then Harry's, and I didn't see that joy and excitement. I wondered what was wrong, such as if perhaps they felt guilty because my father wasn't there. I couldn't believe after everything my father had given her, that she would deprive him of a traditional coat of arms, and go forward with the wedding, knowing that his credibility been destroyed, and that she sat in her pulpit, arrogantly watching it happen, and did nothing to help him. I wondered what the whole procession would have looked like, had my father merely complied. After Meghan and Harry exchanged vows, and were riding away with the crowd, hopefully, and blindly cheering them on, I felt sorry that those who knew the truth, would remember the event as a bad dream. I could only imagine how Trevor would feel watching the wedding, after he had reportedly stated in an interview, that he felt like gum on a shoe. I wondered at that moment, if one day Harry would feel like a piece of gum on a glass slipper. Several men were likely not overflowing with joy, on my sister's wedding day; my father, Trevor, Corey, and Piers Morgan. Rumor had it that my sister was introduced to others who could connect her with Prince Harry, by Piers Morgan, who is a well-connected British morning show host. The line of people who loved, supported and helped her, and whom were ghosted was spreading its wings.

The Urban Dictionary grew a bit when it added the phrase being Meghan Markle'd. It states that, "Meghan Markle is a verb for ghosting or disposing of people once you have no use or benefit from them, without regard to genuine human relationship." As I read that, it felt tragically funny being the first born Markle under my father, and having also been, Meghan Markle'd by my sister. What all of these men had in common, including my father, was that they were all normally handsome, successful, and had spoiled my sister. I doubted they could have foreseen that they would all be feeling similarly, on the day of this historical royal wedding. Watching the sermon in the church, and feeling that my sister turned a deaf ear to the message of it, made me realize that, if religion didn't work to compel her to feel love, gratitude, and compassion for our father and family, then it seemed unlikely that anything would. I was reeling in the thought that, since people are capable of working together to forgive one another when disagreements arise, social labels could be replaced by appreciating people for who they are, regardless of color, religion, disability, or ethnicity. I was overcome by love, hope, and sorrow, over the idea that we could not even treat each other lovingly within the family. I felt that my grandmother would have been disappointed, if she could see how my father was treated after suffering a heart attack, and the wedding proceeding without him. I felt a lot of things, as I looked at the charming television interviewer sitting next to me. I knew he couldn't possibly understand everything I was feeling.

Any faith in reconciliation, that I thought I had, would be completely extinguished over the next two years, as the fairy tale transformed into a tragic comedy. I always said, "Family is capable of surviving everything, or like the old cliché—Love conquers all."

I could only hope for the sake of everyone involved, especially my father, that my sister would realize the family that she always had. I resigned myself to letting go of the sister I once had, but I couldn't fathom what was to come over the next year.

I

To be continued.....

About the Author

Born in Chicago in the 1960's and raised in Southern California, Samantha Markle is an author, screenwriter and counselor. Having battled MS in a wheelchair for most of her adult life, she's no stranger to challenges, or tenacity. With one screenplay in pre-production, and her first book completed, she continues to roll uphill as a squeaky wheel, to defend the truth, and inspire others to look beyond social labels and fake news, to understand who we are as people.

Meg, London England,
(2018 shutter stock photos)

My all-time favorite picture of Meg with me, at my apartment in Westwood, California - 1984

(in my family photo album courtesy of Thomas W. Markle, Sr.)

My Darling, Noel

Printed in Great Britain
by Amazon

58757868R00159